De-Cluttered School

Also available from Continuum

Display for Learning – Kirstie Andrew-Power and Charlotte Gormley

100 Ideas for Essential Teaching Skills – Neal Watkin and Johannes Ahrenfelt

100 Ideas for Teaching Citizenship – Ian Davies

100+ Ideas for Teaching Creativity – Stephen Bowkett

100+ Ideas for Teaching Thinking Skills – Stephen Bowkett

The De-Cluttered School

How to create a cleaner,
calmer and greener
learning environment

Jane C. Anderson

continuum

Thank you to everyone who has contributed to this book and to those I have directly and indirectly learned from. A full list of acknowledgments is included but may I take this opportunity to apologize to anyone whom I may have inadvertently missed. Please contact my publisher if this is the case and I will do my best to ensure the mistake is corrected in further editions.

Continuum International Publishing Group
The Tower Building   80 Maiden Lane, Suite 70
11 York Road   New York, NY 10038
London
SE1 7NX

www.continuumbooks.com

© Jane C. Anderson 2010

British Library Cataloguing-in-Publication Data
A catalogue record for this book is available from the British Library
ISBN: 978-0-82643-139-4 (paperback)

Library of Congress Cataloging in Publication Data
A catalog record for this book has been applied for from the Library of Congress

Typeset by Ben Cracknell Studios
Printed and bound in Great Britain by Bell & Bain, Glasgow

Contents

Acknowledgments

To Bill and Mum and Dad for always being there and bolstering me when (frequently) I need it.

To Eve and William, Katie, Thomas and little William for distracting me from my work and making me smile when I think of them.

To the following people for their contributions, encouragement and feedback: Shirley Clarke, Kim Cowie, Dawn Foster, Dr Barry Hymer, Sir John Jones, Peter McIntosh, Domonic Mulcahy, Bryan Redhead, Helen Walker, Mick Waters, Alice Witherow and, especially Sue Palmer – a kindred spirit. I'm very grateful.

To Bridget Gibbs at Network Continuum Education, for bearing with me and offering me such good advice in the first instance.

To Gateshead Library Service: ever ready to help and always professional.

To Gateshead Council Raising Achievement Service for their all-round support and promotion of my wellness work with schools.

To Greenside School, Wandsbeck First School, Benton Park Primary School and all the other schools and organizations I have worked with over the years, for becoming so wholeheartedly involved in wellness.

And for their friendship, support and gratifying curiosity about my work: Alan, Barbara, Christine, Ednie, Emma, George, Helen, Jane, John, Karen, Kris, Mary, Paul, Phil, Sara, Sharon, Susan, Tim, Tony and Viv. You know who you are. Thank you.

Foreword

An environment that speaks

What's the link between the environment of the school and learning? Well, if you ask most adults about the types of personal qualities that children should develop they will use terms such as confident, inquisitive, self-motivated and organized.

A good classroom should speak to the learner about learning. If history is the label on the door, then the room should ooze history: artefacts, document, photographs, maps. It should speak about the impact of history on society and the value of history to the individual. A mathematics room should promote creativity, pattern and proof. There should be pictures of famous mathematicians as examples of the impact of mathematics on society and pictures of ex students from the school who went on to do mathematics-related work as adults.

In a generic classroom, messages about learning will abound. Research, wonder, exposition and solution will be there to prompt the inquisitive mind.

As for organized and confident minds – well, how we sort the room can help or hinder. To help children learn to be organized the room needs to be tidy, ordered, disciplined, logical and arranged. All effective workshops, whether the local garage or the operating theatre, have uncluttered spaces, good storage and understood routines. So should the learning workshop: the classroom. It extends further: the corridors, the hall, the library, the staircases, the stairwells, outside. This is what the de-cluttered school is all about: recognizing the need for clarity and space as a prerequisite for good quality learning. Once that's established (and this book leaves no stone unturned in showing you how to do so) other factors can be introduced. If we would like children to be caring, thoughtful and sensitive, for instance, we can give them things to look after, things such as plants, pets – even other people.

After all that, it is a matter of letting in some fresh air and getting the right-sized chair with the right-sized table, making sure everyone can see . . . and, of course, teaching really well.

Mick Waters, Professor of Education,
University of Wolverhampton, UK.

Definitions

Clutter clearing: as it sounds; to clear clutter and unwanted goods from any identified space

Get rid of: in this context means to choose from a host of different means of disposal as identified in Chapter 3 (including recycling)

Future investment: spending that might be out of the question at this point but which could be factored into projected outlay at a later date

Subconscious/unconscious: subconscious, as used here, means other brainwork that is going on while the conscious is focusing elsewhere. As opposed to unconscious, which means, here, no *obvious* 'awakeness' at all (as in being hit on the head)

School/learning environment/setting: includes indoor and outdoor spaces used by children to learn and teachers to teach

Feng shui: the study of nature and the environment and the effects they have on the prosperity (health and wealth) of human beings at any given time and place

Introduction

About this book

I have been working in education and training for almost 30 years. For much of that time I have had a simultaneous career as a feng shui practitioner and writer. Over the last few years I have had the opportunity to meld these two strands of my life together and have been assisting not only schools but also organizations as diverse as IKEA, the Police and the National Health Service with various wellness initiatives. The commonality between them is their keen interest in the enrichment of the lives of their employees through better quality work settings. This is where my particular emphasis on enhancing the physical learning and working environment comes into its own. Within this process the cleaning and clearing discussion always engenders the most attention and enthusiasm. Quite simply, organizations – especially schools – cannot have enough clutter clearing but for various reasons they need support in carrying it out. Thanks to my feng shui background I understand the need for clarity and cleanliness in any location, not just the educational setting, and repeatedly see what a massive difference it can make to morale and effectiveness when implemented on a day-to-day basis: hence this book. I would love to help every school with this issue but cannot, so am writing *The De-Cluttered School* to enable schools to do the job themselves. Of course there is no secret to clutter clearing; it just helps to have a few objective guidelines, which this book attempts to provide.

> For many teachers their environment is still a blind spot: unchanging, unchangeable and beyond their control – an obstacle that they must work around, rather than a tool to support and enhance their practice. Design Council, 2005

The first part of the book shows schools how to clutter clear. It gives the reasons, answers the queries and provides a step-by-step guide to the big clutter-clearing day.

The second part is about maintaining the good work. It suggests collecting and acting on feedback, keeping people interested and active, and enabling students to become motivated by making tidiness fun (or fashionable depending on which age group you are dealing with). This section also encompasses storage, display and signage around schools.

The final part is about building on your progress. As little hard evidence is available to prove the effectiveness of a good clear out other than the experiential word of students and teachers working joyfully and more efficiently as a result of it, schools might like to join in helping to prove the case. Sound action research will enable us to eventually promote integrated cleanliness in schools as a solid, accepted holistic practice that happens as a matter of course in every school. Organizations as diverse as The Campaign to Protect Rural England to local authority cleansing departments are also interested in extending this initiative to create a clean and tidy environment beyond the school gates.

Winston Churchill famously said in his address to the nation regarding the re-building of the Houses of Parliament after their destruction during World War II, 'First we shape our places, then they shape us', so let us get on and allow our environment do just that.

What schools say about clutter clearing …

'The clutter clear has made such a difference. I feel like I can breathe now.'

'Before we couldn't move for all the rubbish. Now there seems to be so much space!'

'It was good fun getting rid of so much stuff. I'm looking forward to doing it again.'

'The organization allowed me to concentrate on the job in hand. A whole day to do nothing but sort out was a luxury – and an enjoyable one.'

'I like to clutter clear at home and had always been frustrated by not being able to do the same at work.'

'Some people found it a bit difficult to begin clearing but they seemed to get into it with some support.'

'Everyone mucked in – even the children. And they seem to be more aware of clutter now. I hope we can continue all this.'

'Very cathartic. I went straight home and started there too!'

'I think all schools should do it. The cleaners can get round properly now.'

'Why didn't we clutter clear before? Doing it like this took a lot of preparation but look at what we've achieved.'

'Best staff training day ever! Time spent really usefully.'

'The atmosphere is now tangibly cleaner – and the school has a flow that really wasn't there before.'

This feedback and much, much more like it has been derived from the training and consultation on clutter clearing and enhancing the school environment I have been delivering to schools for many years. The comments always tend to be very similar, such is the satisfaction people feel after they have confronted their mess and cleared their space.

People and their clutter

Most people are pretty clutter-aware in their homes these days but, when it comes to the workplace, the responsibility always seems to fall to someone else. People are interested in a clean and tidy working environment but shared rooms and community areas mean vast tracts of space fall into No Man's Land. Now and again some public-spirited individual will have a go at clearing up but eventually gives up, disillusioned that he or she seems to be the only one making an effort.

Nowhere can this be more the case than schools. So much space and equipment is co-owned, so many materials are allocated to teams rather than individuals, so little storage is available to tuck away valuable things for private safekeeping; it's no wonder that people throw up their hands in despair of ever being able to create any semblance of clarity out of the chaos that schools succumb to so quickly.

One of the main issues with school clutter is that of ownership. If no one claims responsibility for the bits and pieces lying around, how can a decision be taken as to whether or not it is relevant any more? How does anyone know whether to toss it out or keep it?

Much of the problem also has to do with laudable professional thrift. Teaching materials and equipment cost money. Most teachers are highly conscious of this and would rather reuse than spend again, so naturally want to hang onto 'things' for 'next time' or 'just in case'; except, of course there is very little room around schools in which to store such odds and ends. These are the three-legged chairs found teetering at the end of corridors, the deflated footballs rotting in office corners and the odd boots perched on top of classrooms cupboards.

Handmade materials and display pieces are even worse. Often lovingly crafted, they are prized and cherished examples of a teacher's work and hang around, often for years, on the off-chance they might again become useful. And sometimes they are, staying in use from the word go until they literally disintegrate through the handling of hundreds of curious hands. More commonly, sadly, they molder away, forgotten, adding to the general scholastic hubris of faded sugar paper, dented papier-mâché and dust mites. If they've been taken home for safekeeping, a similar demise occurs whereby they end up clogging the attic or spare room until their creator eventually retires and/or moves home.

Then there's the detritus accumulated as a result of the empire building that happens so often in all workplaces, not only schools. A new initiative brings with it kudos for the member of staff tasked to it and piles of associated materials which their new importance gives them leave to deposit willy-nilly around the workplace regardless of anyone else. Later, when the initiative has passed, the materials remain tucked away on the off-chance that they might be useful again. It never happens.

Of course we are all potential hoarders; some people just deal with it better than others. There are numerous theories to explain this squirrelling tendency. Some researchers theorize that we are attached to our things as a result of 'hard-wiring' in our brains which enabled us to survive during the hunter-gatherer period when we had to stockpile food to make it last. In a number of instances hoarding is the result of anxiety and insecurity, which can eventually lead to obsession and compulsive behaviour. Occasionally it is the result of illness or damage which has affected the decision-making part of the brain and impinged on its ability to process information properly.

One of the most interesting schools of thought pertaining to the UK and much of mainland Europe and the old Eastern bloc countries is that we hoard as a result of deprivation experienced during the two world wars. Food and clothing, most things in fact, were in extremely short supply during the early first half of the last century; people in mainland Europe were often hungry. In Britain, during World War II, there was constant trepidation that the same might happen. People reused and held onto *everything*, unsure when it might come their way again. Times were desperate and people deeply frightened. Once the war was over, when people might have expected the situation to relax, it simply got worse. Rationing increased, with all the best goods produced being sold abroad to bring money into the economy. There was little money for the British people to buy anything and not much to buy anyway, and so the populace had to make do and mend.

This kind of conditioning does not disappear quickly. Most west and east European families still remember people hoarding paper bags, bits of string, butter paper, anything that might come in handy or be useful. Potting sheds and kitchen cupboards were full of these things. It was recycling before recycling became fashionable. But for these people it was not a lifestyle choice, it was an indispensable survival skill. Hard learned and never really forgotten, it became a part of the psyche and has had long lasting effects.

A recent art installation from China demonstrates that this affliction is actually a human and global one. Zhao Xiangyuan, a survivor of the Chinese Cultural Revolution (1966–76), applied the philosophy of *wu jin qi jong* – 'waste not' – quite literally and threw away nothing thereafter. The resulting enormous collection of junk was later turned into a staggering memorial to one woman's thrift and trepidation, which was originally shown at Gwangju Biennial in 2006 and most recently at the Museum of Modern Art (New York) in 2009.

Generations later, people still seem in conflict over the whole issue of the accumulation and disposal of possessions. Today it seems all spaces – at home, work and leisure – in Britain are overfilled and over crowded with 'stuff'. We get a thrill from buying something new but are reluctant to throw away the old, so we hang onto it all in blithe denial at the amount of space and energy it consumes. This issue is a huge one and affects us all, but it needs rigorous discussion and deliberate action if we are to begin tackling our mess. And where better to start than schools – which, after all, are places of example? Clutter impinges and influences us in many obvious and insidious ways. But accumulation is only a habit, one that can be moderated like anything else. It begins with having an awareness of our own thoughts and actions and believing that we have some choice in the matter. An understanding as to how clutter is undermining us on a moment by moment basis is helpful.

Why environment matters

Ancient thinking: environment is profoundly important and affects the health and prosperity of human beings all the time.

Recent past thinking: external physical circumstances have no effect on the attitude and behaviour of human beings. Changes in people can only come from within (the self).

Current thinking: cells react and respond to changes in their environment (signal transduction). People can experience physiological improvements and act differently in better quality environments.

Most of us have a day-to-day purpose. Anything that beckons us from that purpose is not usually of immediate value. Clutter constitutes a regular and insidious beckoner, distracting us from our purpose and demoralizing us via each of the senses, eventually overwhelming us with its ubiquity. But clutter usually builds up slowly over a period of time, enabling us to get used to it. In fact it begins to create a cocoon, smothering us with the security of the known. Gradually we become comfortable with the muddle until, one day, we realize that while we cannot live *with* all the tat, we are afraid, for some reason, to live without it. However, by now concentration and creativity have stultified and we find ourselves in a rut. To 'see' our way clear and out of this rut we need space to think and move, but space is the one thing missing in a chaotic environment. It needs to be recreated. This is where a clutter clear comes into its own.

Of course no one gets into such a mess on purpose; no one deliberately goes out one day and decides to bring home or take into work a load of rubbish. Often we do not even notice the build-up until we experience the place in question from a different perspective or someone else points it out to us. Even then we initially jump to its defence, championing the cause of the old musical instrument catalogue, the dried out felt-tips, the ancient trainers. These things feel like trusted friends and disposal of them, a betrayal. It takes a while for logic to oust this strange emotional attachment to our debris but in most cases it does eventually happen, although in a school the problem can be more complex and the solution more protracted. Sometimes a clutter mentality affects a whole department and occasionally whole schools succumb to the malaise, particularly if there has been a period of high staff turnover or some other major confidence-undermining problem. The resultant debacle is a kind of passive aggressive giving-up which eventually fans out to affect a very important and impressionable client group: pupils. They deserve more. Actually everyone in school does and it is something everyone can do something about. This book will show you how to clear your way to the future you want.

You can make your school into a friend or foe. The choice is yours.

The living school

Imagining that, instead of being only a building, your school is human, allows you to view it differently. But what kind of person would it be?

- nagging, undermining and exhausting (as a building – dirty, cluttered and hard work)? The kind of person you avoid? or
- welcoming, happy and hopeful (as a building – clean, orderly and accommodating)? The kind of person you look forward to bumping into?

You can make your school into a friend or foe. The choice is yours.

Where are we now?

'Getting there', would probably be the best way to describe our progress towards really appropriate and tangibly supportive learning environments. The following quote, although referring to the UK, no doubt sums up the position of most schools not only in Europe or even the West but globally, '… many educators occupy environments they are unable to exploit to the fullest. Many children and young people, too, spend much of their time in drab and hindering environments that they learn to "tune out" of rather than develop an awareness and sense of belonging' (Clark, 2002).

School design is once again a hot topic, which can only be good news for teachers and learners fortunate enough to be in line for a rebuild. Yet the majority of people in schools today still make their way to a structure that is simply not fit for purpose: often an inefficient Victorian building or derivative interpretation of 60s open-plan architecture. These buildings, although sometimes interesting in themselves, are often difficult to clean, heat, cool, and move around and teach in. However, modernization is expensive, disruptive and frequently exclusive, as, despite lip service to school users, heed is still insufficiently paid to their needs in the end.

Why clutter clearing is the in-thing

Clutter clearing, in comparison with the drawn-out and the sometimes dubious luxury of re-build, is:

- immediate
- effective – what you end up with afterwards is always better than what you had before
- cheap
- very satisfying
- inclusive and a great whole school team builder.

Everyone can be involved for next to nothing, have great fun and make a huge impact on their environment. Yet most schools are still not partaking of this wonderful phenomenon. Things are changing, however, and, as they join in, schools will become freer, more relaxed, more healthy and a joy for everyone to learn and work in. So roll up your sleeves and enjoy yourselves!

Yet things are improving, with the immediate school environment increasingly being recognized for the difference it can make to everyone within it. As Dr Barry Hymer, Still Thinking founder and Visiting Fellow at Newcastle University's Centre for Teaching and Learning, points out, 'The physical learning environment often plays the Cinderella role to her big sisters – the cognitive, emotional and social learning spaces. When this happens, they're all diminished. The physical learning space deserves an equal emphasis if we're to aspire to a complete, rich and healthy learning environment. She too must go to the ball.'

Of course, Cinderella must go to the ball. Reggio Emilia educators (schools established after World War II to focus pre- and primary school education on the philosophy of the principles of respect, responsibility and community, through exploration and discovery) also stress that the environment can motivate children, enhance learning and reduce behaviour problems. Cornell University Environmental and Developmental Psychologist Dr Gary Evans' research shows that effects of the physical environment – noise level, overcrowding, housing and neighbourhood quality – affect children's cognitive development as significantly as

The environment can motivate children, enhance learning and reduce behaviour problems.

psychosocial relationships (for more about Gary Evans' research see: www.human. cornell.edu/che/bio.cfm?netid=gwe1). His colleague at the same university, Lorraine Maxwell, Associate Professor of Design and Environmental Analysis, agrees saying that children are socialized as much by their physical environments as they are by the people in their lives (Maxwell, 2007). Her findings have also shown that children's personal and academic growth is 'directly connected to the conditions in the classroom and home' (Ulrich, 2004).

Teachers need to be particularly aware of the values they are subconsciously displaying in all areas of their professional life including their appearance, behaviour and use of personal space, as children will always be noticing and learning from them. Teachers who are scruffy and surrounded by clutter will project completely different messages about self-respect and the importance of their work from the teachers who keep on top of themselves and their classroom.

The fact that we are always making an impression is something that simply cannot be ignored. Neutral teaching is not possible in the same way that neutral living and being in a neutral space are not possible. Everything around us gives us direct and indirect messages all the time; as we

Neutral teaching is not possible in the same way that neutral living and being in a neutral space are not possible.

are doing to them. The greater the exposure to the same messages, the more repeated the emphasis and the deeper the imprint created.

Think how often you and the children you teach enter and make use of the school environment. Day in, day out you are all exposing yourselves to the same messages. What are they? Do they reinforce the values you espouse in assembly or from the front of your classroom? Are you giving good verbal advice only to be undermined by a bad example of the Almighty Wall, as Edward Thring, the influential nineteenth century headteacher of Uppingham School, in Rutland, called the school building? Do you advocate inclusion but display only the work of the few? Do you talk about reduce, reuse and recycle but surround yourself with a sea of unwanted and undealt-with stuff?

Nothing is more confusing to children than adults who say one thing and do another. Congruity in all forms is fundamental to the quality of messages that children receive, be they directly from guiding adults or indirectly through their spaces and places, i.e. home, school and 'third place' physical settings. It is not good enough to say one thing and do another. Strength, honesty, resilience, respect and so on are values that can and should be displayed in all human manifestations, including the design, decoration and maintenance of our buildings. Adults who drop litter and waste materials but preach order and thrift teach only hypocrisy and contempt for the physical world. Spaces (including schools) that are uncared for and dirty are likely to teach only exhaustion and hopelessness.

The fact is that indirect environmental teaching is happening anyway, so why not make use of it and incorporate it as a considered and supportive element of the teaching and learning experience? Make the decision to live as you teach and teach as you live. Wherever possible, let the spaces you inhabit speak the same message as you. Let your life and world flow as one as much as you can and allow your students to experience through you the peace that comes from integrity (living a whole, non-conflicted life). After all, if you don't demonstrate it, the majority of children will never have another chance to learn it. Like it or not, in the end that's what being a teacher of children is all about.

But what are teachers taught?

Many academics and practitioners apparently agree that environment counts. So where is it on the teacher training curriculum? Very much in the small print at most institutions, if research into this field is to be believed. Lackney and Jacobs (2002) comment, 'Many teachers and administrators tend to focus on pedagogical and interpersonal issues, ignoring the physical–spatial context in which the teaching–learning process occurs [Loughlin and Suina, 1982; Weinstein, 1981]. The physical environment of the classroom is often neglected as an integral component of the instructional design that should reflect learning objectives and teaching methods'.

Lackney and Jacobs conclude in this study that teachers' pre-service training does not prepare them for the challenges of making the physical classroom setting complimentary to the curriculum. These teachers relied instead, it seems, on trial and error experiential methods to develop a cogent set of design principles intrinsic to their teaching style and teaching context. Surely this reinventing of the wheel by generation after generation of teachers is an utter waste of time.

Loughlin and Suina (1982) also note that teachers and administrators tend to focus more in the first instance on pedagogy and communications rather than the spaces where these happen. Johnson (1973) attributes a lack of clarity in the physical, social and psychological factors that make the total environment to '... the general tendency of educators to ignore or *outright reject* the role the environment might play in the dynamics of learning or teaching' (author's emphasis).

Winifred Gallagher, in her book *The Power of Place* (1994), interestingly comments on this still prevalent viewpoint resulting from Freudian theory which places great emphasis on the importance of a person's internal psychological processes, heavily shaped by the past, in determining his or her 'way of being'. She goes on to suggest that, 'Freudians were sceptical of the idea that altering one's milieu, say, where one lived, might also have merit. That kind of thing was, they said, "running away from your problems," even though the people who ran away sometimes felt better.'

Further, 'By promoting a false dichotomy between the influences of biology and environment – often narrowly interpreted as meaning only the social setting – academe has also helped obscure the synchrony between behaviour and it's milieu.' This is changing though. 'The study of molecular genetics, for example, reveals that what a cell will be is determined, not just by what is in it but also by who its neighbours are; through various constituents it is sensitive to, the gene's microenvironment influences its workings,' i.e. space counts. It *does* have an effect and it *should* be addressed in terms of its potential as a learning tool.

Rodney D. Fulton, in his proposal for SPATIAL (satisfaction-participation-achievement-transcendent-immanent-attributes-authority-layout, 1991), a model for understanding the physical attributes of learning environments, noted in his research that, 'Finkel (1984) called for "learning-engineered" environments because "if we specify the environment completely enough, we can predict human behavior exactly"'.

The findings are out there. Getting them meaningfully incorporated into teacher training has yet to happen in any widespread, meaningful way.

Never the less, progress is happening, gradually; building design is improving, every so often; interior design gets better, in some places; usage and maintenance are gaining in profile. But interest in what can be done immediately, to incentivize people in school right now through their environment, still needs great attention.

1

Six good reasons to clear your school

- Begin a life habit for children and have a wonderful effect on the world
- Cultivate whole school wellness
- Revitalize the classroom
- Inspection meets the environment criteria and more
- Breathe better – beat the bugs and bacteria
- How clutter clearing ticks the boxes

These six reasons should more than justify an immediate scrum for bin bags and individual schools will probably have their own issues too, all of which will probably be improved by a good clear out. Economy is a common one: many schools have so much stuff that they cannot see the wood for the trees and end up re-buying things they already have but don't know they have as they cannot find them. However, the above reasons can be used as a starting point in persuading most parties in school that a clutter clear is well overdue.

Words of wisdom

If you are in any further doubt about the direct impact of the school environment and the effect it can have, note these words from some the most innovative, successful and enduring educationalists and childcare experts of our time:

The environment is an extra teacher (Reggio Emilia).

First the education of the senses, then the education of the intellect (Maria Montessori [1870–1952], whose education methods allowed students from pre-school to adolescence to develop skills at a pace they set – 'spontaneous self-development').

> We never educate directly, but indirectly by means of the environment
> (John Dewey [1859–1952], one of the twentieth century's most
> influential educationalists).
>
> The human being is a product of his environment (Shinichi Suzuki
> [1898–1998] a self-taught violinist who taught music using a
> pedagogical philosophy, 'mother tongue', in which children learn
> through observation of their environment and a love of life).
>
> Children learn and remember at least as much from the context of the
> classroom as from the content of the coursework (Lawrence Kutner,
> a clinical psychologist and child development writer).

Begin a life habit for children and have a wonderful effect on the world

The title of this section sounds very politically active, almost ridiculously far-reaching and quaintly old fashioned in its goodly intentions. Yet, interestingly, giving children the tools (knowledge and skills) to create order and initiating them into the intellectual and emotional benefits of tidiness make common sense on so many levels. To live cleanly and economically and feel part of a fresh and hopeful world is an achievable ideal that will incite within them the impetus to ultimately change the very land in which they live and their planet beyond that.

Beginning in school (assuming it has not already begun in the home) children will be able to carry their tidy habit with them everywhere. They will know how to create clarity where they live, contribute to cleanliness in the street and impress with their environmental conscientiousness while travelling.

As growing citizens with a heightened awareness of civic responsibility, children will choose reduced packaging, throw less away, recycle where possible and demand more from local government in terms of aesthetic and hygienic pride, e.g. the emptying of overflowing waste bins, properly implemented litter fines, etc. The wider and on-going effects of this are profound. Many places in the world today are not materially poor but they are often astoundingly filthy. Britain is one, although moves are being made to improve the situation, most vociferously by Bill Bryson, American writer and champion of British towns and countryside and President of the Campaign for the Protection of Rural England, who never loses an opportunity to point out what we have and how lucky we are to have it. America is another, although some states are better at cleaning up than others. Clutter clearing in school can help support and underpin a whole cultural programme of integrated environmental awareness and responsible behaviour.

Teaching children how to demonstrate respect for the space and objects around them is a fundamental human duty. We should all be modelling and supporting such respect whenever and wherever we can. If we have not been doing so, we can start now, not only in our schools but throughout our lives, and immediately begin to shape the difference we want to see in our society.

> Let me remind you of an important fact: nowhere in the world is there a landscape more lovely to behold, more comfortable to be in, more artfully worked, more visited and walked across and gazed upon than the countryside of England. It is a glorious achievement and much too lovely to trash. (Bryson, 2009)

Cultivate whole school wellness

> Everything around you is calling to you; everything is telling you a story. Make sure it's a good one. (Purr, 2001)

Tidiness and clarity cost nothing, yet when put in place they allow for something special to happen: space of mind. This happens when all distractions have been removed from our awareness: both conscious and subconscious. It gives us a kind of physiological breathing space in which to allow long ignored or repressed thoughts and feelings to surface and be noticed. Often our lives are so full of diversions on a day-to-day basis that we tend not to have time for contemplation, to simply be still – in fact many people are nervous of 'the quiet' in the same way others are of 'the dark'. However, constant stimulation, which is what many people are habituated to, eventually becomes exhausting. We need to respect our senses and rest them as we do our physical body or at least provide some contrast for them. Unfortunately, in our society the senses are being beckoned to all the time and rarely get the sort of 'down time' needed to relax and recharge.

While conscious, we cannot switch off from being able to see, hear, feel, taste and smell. It is always happening either directly, or on the periphery while we are getting on with other things. This peripheral stimulation affects our thoughts and feelings on a moment-by-moment basis. Barry Lopez underlined this in his work *Crossing Open Ground* (1989) when he wrote, 'The interior landscape responds to the character and subtly of the exterior landscape; the shape of the individual mind is affected by land as it is by genes.'

Feng shui points out that everything around us is eliciting our attention all the time and that, as this is happening anyway, we may as well ensure that we benefit from the sensory stories we are experiencing rather than be depleted or distracted by them.

To benefit we need to carefully reconsider *everything* around us in any given place (in this case a school) and ensure it is imparting something – a message – we perceive to be positive and supportive. Support for this comes from the work of Caine and Caine (1997) when they pointed out that thoughts, emotions, imagination, predisposition and physiology operate concurrently and interactively as the entire system interacts and exchanges information with its environment.

Space and a certain relaxed order seem to be what most people find most helpful in educational settings. Clutter and dirt, which distract from this ideal, should of course be avoided. They crowd in and undermine, detracting from the messages of calm and flow, dignity and joy that most schools wish to inculcate. Space around us creates space in the mind from which new thoughts and dreams, questions and solutions can seed and spread.

Revitalize the classroom

Each day over 53 million school children and six million adults – 20 per cent of the entire USA population – enter the nation's 120,000 school buildings to teach and learn. Unfortunately, in too many cases they enter 'unclean school buildings' that undermine education, health and attendance. According to the US Environmental Protection Agency:

> Studies show one half of the nation's schools have problems linked to indoor air quality. Students, teachers and staff are at greater risk because of the hours spent in school facilities and because children especially are susceptible to pollutants. Schools are also more densely populated and more intensively used than commercial offices for adults, another contributor to the overall problem. This comes at a time when six million school-age children are afflicted with asthma ... and lose approximately 14 million school days annually as a result of asthma. (Barnett, 2006)

These statistics are shocking and avoidable, or at least reducible, and shifting unwanted clutter is the first step towards enabling this to happen. Making space allows better quality cleaning to take place and fresher premises reduce the opportunity for infections to thrive and bacteria to breed. Also, once a space has been properly cleared and thoroughly cleaned, it becomes open to interpretation. What do you want this space to say about learning to its occupants thereafter? How often do you want it repeated? What kind of emphasis would you prefer? What colours do you want to use? How do you want it to smell; what will it sound like?

De-clutter and you'll have the chance to really consider all the sensory storytellers in your classroom. Once empty of distractions, you will be able to address each peripheral source of information individually and recreate its impact, thereafter ensuring its subliminal support for the overt message you are delivering as you teach. As has been said before, learning loss occurs where learning is not sufficiently embedded, supported or encouraged by, in this context, the learning environment. Anne Taylor, Professor of Architecture, University of New Mexico with over 20 years experience in the field of design for learning environments, agrees, stating categorically, 'That there cannot be a separation between the learning process and the physical environment – they are integral parts of each other' (1991). Saeki (Saeki et al., 1995) agrees, 'Learning in broad sense is a process of accessing culture via constant interactions with mediators in the surrounding environment: people, artefacts and settings.' Yet not so many mediators as to allow the effects become bewildering! Begin with 'less is more' and work up from there.

5S

The clarity and vision that emerge from regular clearing and ordering are not unique to education. 5S is a Japanese philosophical system that increases competitive edge in the workplace by refining and managing for better safety standards, reduced waste, improved work flow and enhanced staff morale. Transliterated and translated, the 5S methodologies are as follows: ⇨

1 sort and straighten
2 set locations and limits
3 shine and visually sweep
4 standardize
5 sustain/self-discipline.

Albert Einstein also believed in something similar. According to him there are three rules of work: out of clutter find simplicity; from discord find harmony; and in the middle of difficulty lies opportunity. His words still hold true. This way of working seems to have been re-invented with each generation but from culture to culture, age to age, the basic tenets for best human functioning – be it work, learn or play – seem to remain the same: clear environments produce clearer thinking, happier people and more effective action.

Simply getting classrooms properly cleared out in the first instance is an achievement in itself. Not so much to ask for, you might think, a clean room in which to teach and learn, but consider the number of school spaces where this basic requirement simply cannot be realized and you begin to appreciate its importance. Minimizing the build-up of equipment and materials and avoiding clutter will go a long way towards the creation and maintenance of this ideal and at the same time allow cleaning staff proper access. Thereafter, the classroom is almost your oyster. Anything you bring into this space hereon will have an immediate impact for the first couple of weeks. Then it will call to occupants at a peripheral, subconscious rather than direct level (although still having a subtle, profound effect).

Take one sense at a time and look at the options for it. Remember each sense can become cluttered of itself. Consider walking through a perfumery department and being overwhelmed by the sheer number of scents you encounter, the disorientation that arises from the sudden onslaught of noise when entering a nightclub or the taste confusion that comes from loading your plate up at a buffet.

With careful thought as to what is to be replaced, re-sited and newly designed in the classroom, you can greatly influence the education of any group. Learners will be subliminally absorbing everything around them as you teach, ensuring the frontline message is underpinned by 360 degree support of the setting itself. As Charles Spence, Professor of Experimental Psychology at Oxford University, says in his fascinating *ICI Report on the Secrets of the Senses* (2002):

'Our appreciation of the immediate environment may be subconscious, but this makes it no less crucial to the way we perform.'

Inspection: meet the environment criteria and more

A report by PriceWaterhouseCoopers (PWC, 2003), commissioned by the then Department of Education and Employment (DfEE), noted, 'Recent Ofsted reports have stated that as many as one in five schools in England have accommodation that is in such an unsatisfactory state that the delivery of the curriculum is affected.' This state of affairs is changing, but extremely slowly.

School inspectors make mandatory reference to the 'environmental dimension of schools' during their visits. This term is used to include both the curriculum and the *context in which it is delivered*, i.e. the school building and grounds. Cluttered and unkempt schools certainly give an impression of neglect, and are certainly not evidence of 'the physical environment promoting wellbeing'.

There are several areas of the English Ofsted Inspection Framework under Evidence of the Environmental Dimension where a school with a history of integrated clutter clearing and a school clutter policy will be likely to score over those that do not. For more see Table 1.1.

Why our favourite places are favourite

Where do you like to go? What are some of your most preferred built environments? Which stores, art galleries, cafes, hairdressers, museums, hospitals, etc. do you like to be in? Why? Have you ever considered what thoughts and feelings are generated by these places? Most people tend to avoid grubby, crowded, confusing, dull, stagnant, places in favour of those with natural light, space, clarity, pleasant scent, interesting surfaces, conducive decor, relaxed ambiance and pleasant sounds. This is unsurprising. The latter environment is one much more likely to help us thrive as human beings. It involves all our senses, keeping us alert and subtly motivated. Naturally, intrinsically seeking health, we gravitate towards such a state. This sense of vitality needs to be translated into the school environment so everyone can benefit from it on a daily basis.

Comments from school inspectors about school buildings and grounds

It is important for the sake of the whole school community that school leadership place emphasis upon a healthy and inspiring environment. Once this is valued as part of the school's ethos, such awareness will become an integral part of the school's systems, and its effectiveness will be seen at an emotional and academic level. Where this is not happening it may be necessary to break with the traditional approaches and reconsider the learning environment in a new light, if provision and standards are to be improved. (Tim Nelson, Gateshead Council Raising Achievement Service School Inspector)

'Schools and classrooms can be like many people's minds: cluttered and disorganized. When we focus on what we want, we can throw things away that we don't need any more – this is where a more streamlined approach can help in school. Editing the classroom environment, and refining what is left to what is supportive and reassuring rather than distracting', undoubtedly ensures a better quality teaching and learning experience all round. (Helen Walker, School Improvement Adviser and Inspector, Newcastle City Council Children's Services and Regional TDA Lead for 'Building Aspiration, Resilience and Optimism in the Children's Workforce in the North East') (also see www.bouncebackbehappy.com).

> When we focus on what we want, we can throw things away that we don't need any more.

Support for these views comes from the same PWC report (2003) mentioned above, noting, 'The architecture of school building condition and design generally finds a *positive relationship* between the quality of the physical environment and pupil performance.'

Breathe better – beat the bugs and bacteria

Ask any school cleaner what his or her biggest bugbears are about the job and he or she will almost always say, 'Food and stuff', i.e. the ubiquity of the first and the sheer, inhibiting quantity of the latter. A lot of teaching staff in schools complain about the standard of cleaning in their classrooms and other learning areas. They feel it is not good enough and wonder why the job cannot be done 'properly'. After a while they give up, thinking they have developed a kind of immunity to it. They do not. Neither do the children nor anyone else in school. Dirt and mess will always demoralize for the first two or three weeks; later it becomes more insidious and subconscious. It breeds a subtle, niggling irritation that constantly seeks to weaken concentration by repeatedly calling attention to itself and away from the job in hand: in this case, teaching and learning.

But school cleanliness is not just the responsibility of the school maintenance staff. Most school cleaners are frustrated at not being able to do their job as thoroughly as they would like to. In fact, they are physically inhibited by the overwhelming array of display materials, spare furniture and unstored equipment, i.e. clutter. They cannot get behind, under or on top of things to vacuum, dust and wipe as they would like to. Instead they whisk around the centre of the room 'spot vacuuming', leaving all the hard to reach fingerprints, food spills, crumbs and day-to-day detritus to build up into a delightful patina of its own. Eventually most slip into the same apathy that engulfs everyone else in the school and the place becomes dirtier and dirtier.

A day in the life of a school cleaner

It's 6am on a cold, dark winter's morning; it's raining and likely to turn to snow. Over 50,000 people are setting off from home to clean thousands of schools up and down the country.

When they arrive at work they are likely to be met with a crumbling old building: there is still a chill in the air while the antiquated heating slowly rumbles into life. Grit previously put down to deal with the ice outside has been trodden through the corridors.

They get their equipment ready and enter a classroom that has been left as it was from the day before. The room is littered with debris. Paper, pencils and play-dough are strewn over the floor. The tables are covered in glue, paint and writing. There are marks on the walls from the cellotape used in yesterday's projects. So the cleaner has to clear up before they can start their cleaning duties. It is hard work but they take pride in their job; they love the children, staff and the building. When their shift finishes at 8.45am the room is bright and shiny, fresh and hygienic. The cleaner leaves the building after briefly chatting to staff, knowing they will be faced with exactly the same mess tomorrow – and all for £6.20 per hour.

Clutter and pests go hand-in-hand

The biggest potential pest threat in most classrooms is clutter. Pests gravitate towards cluttered areas because clutter enables pests to hide and reproduce undisturbed from predators and people. 'Pest control efforts are impossible in cluttered areas. Should mice, spiders, cockroaches, etc. be embedded among boxes, paper piles and junk, there is very little a pest management professional can do to eliminate the pests. There are no magic sprays, bug bombs or mouse baits that will penetrate cluttered closets or rooms and eliminate hiding pests' (Purdue University, 2002).

Clutter also affects air quality. In the USA more than a quarter of Chicago teachers reported reduced effectiveness due to asthma, and a further 16 per cent cited sinus problems as a result of poor environmental conditions in schools (Schneider, 2003).

Pest Press (2005) supports this saying, 'A cluttered classroom or kitchen, creates barriers to efficiency and many (including students) may

Clutter speak

New terms are arising to deal with our acquiring and hoarding tendencies:

Infonoia – fear of being caught without an important document or paranoia of lack of information (www.whitespace.com) leading to gross reproduction of the same document so there is always one to hand, in turn creating excess paper and clutter and wasting resources.

feel stressed with the informational and visual overload of a cluttered environment. Clutter also contributes to the accumulation of dust and provides harborage for insects. In this way clutter is more than just a stress-inducer; it can be a health concern.' The fact is that a lot schools are very dirty places. They are sweaty, sticky, slimy, smelly, dingy, dusty and downright icky. They attract pests such as mice, rats, flies, cockroaches, ants and lice. They breed moulds and pathogens and collect irritants and allergens. A recent report states that 'It is not uncommon for 2 or 3 families of mice (15–20 mice) to share the base of one cardboard box in a classroom's cluttered closet' (Heiss, 2004). Staff know this, that is why many of them dress as if they are ready for DIY rather than the teaching of young children. Why wear something decent to a job where surfaces are layered in bacteria, and vermin is widespread? Eventually schools need to make a choice: pets or purity.

Advantages of enhanced health and hygiene in school

Air quality – less dust and dirt, more oxygen, better breathing.

Attendance – less sickness all around.

Exercise – less stuff, more room: kids get up, move around and work off some calories.

Fresher surfaces – properly wiped surfaces, fewer itchy and scratchy problems.

Recruitment and retention – obvious really, but staff are attracted to clean and healthy work surroundings.

Safety – better emergency egress particularly for those with sight or walking difficulties.

Vitality – increased physiological wellbeing for everyone; more space and less matter.

Table 1.1 How whole school clutter clearing ticks the boxes

National initiative/ strategy Whole school policy	Clutter clearing helps meet this by
Every Child Matters: be healthy	Physically: enabling healthier classroom and school conditions, i.e. enhancing air quality and general hygiene in the school setting. Encouraging more movement (exercise) around the classroom
Every Child Matters: stay safe	From accidental injury: improving health and safety/creating better access/egress around school for both able bodied/ disabled children
Every Child Matters: enjoy and achieve	Enjoy and attend school: reducing pupil absences due to respiratory and skin complaints. Encouraging attendance by making school a more attractive place to be
Every Child Matters: make a positive contribution	Engage in positive behaviour in and out of school: leading pupils to dispose of litter responsibly and have a regard for their wider environment
Ofsted inspection Evaluating personal development and wellbeing	Learners' treatment of school facilities Trends in attendance and whether it has improved as a result of actions taken by the school The development of learners' understanding of citizenship
Ofsted inspection Evaluating the curriculum and other activities	The extent to which enrichment activities and/or extended services contribute to learners' enjoyment and achievement, and their contribution to the community The extent to which the provision contributes to improvements in learners' personal development
Ofsted inspection	Working with external agencies: participating in national initiatives, i.e. Keep Britain/Scotland/Wales Tidy, Community Hygiene Concern, etc.
Healthy Schools Award	1.7 Working with external agencies: schemes of work reflecting appropriate involvement of outside agencies. Evaluating contributions through action research 4.8 Confidence and self-esteem: allowing children and young people to overtly participate in school clutter clearing policy via curricular and extra-curricular activities, e.g. Tidy Tots, Clutterbusters' Club, Envirominders
Social and emotional aspects of learning	Self-manage behaviour socially, emotionally and in the physical environment, i.e. respect surroundings, both built and natural
Staff evaluation	Encouraging individual clarity, focus, direction and commitment to whole school strategy

National initiative/ strategy Whole school policy	Clutter clearing helps meet this by
Investors in People	Developing strategies to improve the performance of an organization – Whole School Clutter Clearing Policy (Point 1) Taking action to Improve the performance of an organization – via clutter clearing training and day (Point 8) Evaluation of the impact of the performance on the organization – using post-clutter clearing day evaluation (Points 9 and 10)
Governor subcommittee: premises, health and safety	Helping to ensure health and safety issues are met, e.g. risk assessment Contributing to reports on the condition of buildings and school environment
Governor subcommittee: staffing	Ensuring teachers and headteachers can achieve a reasonable work/life balance (Remodelling National Agreement) through an enhanced (cleaner, healthier more organized) working environment
Workforce reform/ remodelling	Managing change: inclusive culture – enabling everyone in school to contribute and play their part in initial clutter clearing and subsequent maintenance Also work/life balance as staffing above
School council and student voice	Life skills: developing citizenship skills including environmental responsibility fostered by school curriculum Improving behaviour: exercising personal tidiness and cleanliness in and beyond the school Building the school community: peer pressure encourages good housekeeping habits initiated via clutter clearing, consequentially enhancing wellbeing for all in school
Extended School Status	Working with voluntary and community sector: see Healthy Schools Award 1.7 above Evaluating and monitoring: on-going action research into increased school 'wellness' as a result of clutter clearing (CC) and implementation of whole school CC policy Use of premises: rationalizing space and capacity post-clutter clearing
Next practice	Communities for Learning: (3) Identifying and working with other organizations within the local and wider community who can support and invest in and benefit from pupils' enhanced respect for their environment

National initiative/ strategy Whole school policy	Clutter clearing helps meet this by
Eco Schools Award	Bronze (b) (e) clutter clearing, recycling and resource management forms part of school environmental review and has been incorporated to some extent within the curriculum
Sustainable schools	Purchasing and waste: whole school recycling during initial clutter clear, refined management of recourses and waste thereafter, e.g. encouraging greater sharing/repair/reuse/ recycling of, etc. Local wellbeing: incorporating clutter awareness and action into curriculum/ broadening pupils' wider regard and respect for their community via school policy and partnership with other conservation and environmental agencies
Rights Respecting School Award (UNICEF)	Article 24: Children have a right to a clean environment. Also, if children have a right to a clean environment, then they also have a responsibility to do what they can to look after their environment
Go4It	Free up teaching and learning in schools encouraging a very different approach to embracing the challenges and opportunities that lay ahead in life. Allow children to participate in clearing and clearing in school, i.e. putting their chair on top of their desk to enable cleaners greater access
Green School Awards	Totally active: whole school clutter clear/litter pick

Case study: the strange case of the marching corridor that thought it was a dumping ground

Greenside Primary School sits on the side of a hill on the outskirts of Greenside village – once a busy mining community. Today the area is thriving again, fast becoming popular as a commutable location for city centre workers, yet it has managed to retain its unpretentious and slightly sleepy character.

The school has two distinct parts: the original Victorian red brick building and a more recent stone extension. The headteacher, Dawn Foster, was concerned about several issues with regard to the building but in particular wanted to marry the two parts more fully so as to give a better feeling of continuity. She also wanted to clear both halves of all the extraneous matter impairing the 'flow' of the school. Most urgent was a marching corridor in the older wing of the school. This was built at the time of the Boer War to allow pupils the opportunity to improve their health by marching up and down what, in fact, was a very wide internal corridor. While it may have been fit for purpose at the time, it was now a bit of a white elephant, filled with boxes and gaping cupboards holding miscellaneous school paraphernalia. Despite this, the space undoubtedly had a gentle charm. There were connotations of the internal 'streets' which architects are so keen on including in commercial and public settings today. The high-domed glass ceiling allowed plenty of overhead, natural light in, from which the adjoining classrooms along each side benefited through their widowed walls. Beneath these ran a dado with highly practical wood panelling below. The floor was wonderfully waxed and had aged parquet. The marching corridor was a place that begged some TLC and in turn it would provide the people using it with the same.

The school began by clearing out all the boxes, papers, and plastic bits and pieces stacked up on the floor around the walls. Then the nasty hardboard panels, which had been tacked over the attractive wood panelling, were torn off. The cupboards standing at both ends (which always stood ajar, highlighting the mess within) were emptied, and then removed. This left an even more wonderful, light-filled space. The display boards were cleared then re-covered in matching backcloth. The work subsequently mounted was properly spaced and spoke of the same subject message throughout. Even the mobiles that hung in the ceiling space were taken down, allowing cleaning staff to get into corners they didn't know existed and the caretaker to retouch paintwork where needed. Doors that had previously stood open, revealing nothing more than dark, jumbled enclaves beyond, were now closed, effectively reforming the shape of the corridor into a sympathetic, balanced rectangle.

The final touches came with the purchase of 12 four-foot parlour palm plants, which were placed at strategic points around the walls. These softened the whole space and were met with delight by both staff and pupils alike. The children were given watering cans and happily took to caring and tending them. As the children entered and exited their classrooms via the corridor it was not uncommon to see them running their fingers softly though the leaves.

The headteacher reported that an unexpected result of the experience was that the children seemed to be much calmer in this area than they had been previously. In respect of this they had decided to cease using the bell, deeming it to be an unnecessarily brutal disruption to the newly created atmosphere of tranquility.

2

Begin with people

No involvement, no commitment!

- Children
- Teaching staff
- Support staff
- Cleaning and maintenance staff
- Senior management teams (including headteachers and bursars)
- Governors
- Parents and PTA
- Other stakeholders
- Case study

The art of diplomacy is allowing the other person to have your way, to paraphrase the Italian diplomat, Daniele Vare. This is still true today. Encouraging the above, sometimes disparate, parties to believe that they all have something gain from filling bin bags on their next training day will take a great deal persuasiveness. Each group has different goals so will need a separate driver or reason for participating. However, they do have one common denominator and that is nature. All things being healthy, our five senses will always respond to nature's stimulants. Regularly exposed to the outdoor environment, our senses become heightened and vitalized. On the other hand, stuffy and hampered internal environments arrest our natural faculties and reduce awareness. Poor environments subdue us, breeding lethargy that manifests itself as a comfort zone of apathy.

Clearing a setting to allow more 'flow' and ease of movement, cleaner surfaces, fragrant spaces and lots of natural light allows users to breathe deeply and flourish.

Often it happens without us realizing. However, a good clear out can rid a building and everyone within it of stultifying attitudes and behaviours. Clearing a setting to allow more 'flow' and ease of movement, cleaner surfaces, fragrant spaces and lots of natural light allows users to breathe deeply and flourish. This end result of a clutter clearing day will benefit all school users and unite them in appreciation of a job well done, although they may find it difficult to articulate quite why it has been so successful. People usually note that 'they feel better' or 'they like being in school more now', and really that is what it is all about, creating a place where people enjoy being.

How does your school manifest itself now? Keep checking progress by using the descriptive lists in Table 2.1.

Table 2.1 Managing the de-cluttered school

Under de-cluttered (stagnant and stressful)	De-cluttered (balanced and healthy)	Over de-cluttered (frenetic and stressful)
Apathetic and unattractive	Friendly and inviting	Cold and intimidating
Ricochets between frenetic and exhausted	Calm and well-paced	Continuously on edge
Lax	Orderly and organized	Regimented
Flaccid	Structured	Inflexible and rigid
Directionless/inconsistent	Consultative	Directive
Anonymous/well-meaning and unavailable	Supportive and accessible	Controlling and unavailable
Indifferent and off-putting	Expansive and open	Distant and closed
Reductive and un/de-motivated	Effective and motivated	Reductive and de-motivated
Lethargic	Comfortable and relaxed	Perfectionist
Indifferent and unconcerned	Inclusive and reassuring	Narrow and alienating
No one cares	Intra/personally accountable	Micromanaged by hierarchy
Indiscernible management	Transformative management	Transactional management
Things never get done	Things are done voluntary	Things are enforced
No option – independency or capitulation	Encourages interdependency	Breeds dependency
De-cluttering unheard of	De-cluttering an integrated whole school process (on-going)	De-cluttering a dreaded drill-like dictate along with clear-desk policy and the like

Children

Why should children muck in with a clutter clear? What is in it for them? Will it be fun? Will there be food? What strategies can be used to persuade them that clearing and tidying are good? What techniques will allow them to get on with it?

These are challenging questions as can be deduced from the reams written about this issue in professional publications, blogs, websites, etc. It causes much hand wringing both at school and in the home, and while a lot of good work has been done in this area, it does not seem to be included in much depth within teacher training programmes, probably due to time pressure and the fact that it is not deemed to be of sufficient academic merit to be included. Professor Maria Montessori made time for it, however. One of the greatest, time-tested educational theorists and practitioners of the last century, she absolutely believed in the 'prepared classroom', the orderly environment she advocated to enable children to feel comfortable and safe. Her research repeatedly showed that most children respond positively to clear boundaries, consistently applied. Within this structure they know where they are: they might not always agree with it but it provides safety, enabling them to relax and focus on learning and play.

Boys tend to react especially well to this arrangement. Being specific with instructions aids them still further. Assuming you actually want to include them in low-level clutter clearing (and there's no reason why they should not be included), tasks can be made more enjoyable by timing them or framing them as a 'tough' or competitive challenge or game. Leave out words pertaining to tidying, clearing or cleaning (unless it is a tank or tractor) in your instructions as they will behave as if the job is beneath them. Instruct, as opposed to request, incorporating words and phrases such as chase after, bunch up, get, build, manoeuvre and plot. Family psychologist and boy's champion Steve Biddulph regularly uses the phrase 'Can you handle that?' to follow non-negotiable conversations with boys of all ages. 'Are you tough enough?' is another to which many will respond as a way of raising their game. Somewhat trite-sounding and apparently stereotypical, this approach does the job surprisingly well. It helps if a respected male is doing the talking and models the required behaviour at the same time. Show boys exactly what debris you want heaped up, give them a trolley or wagon to shift it and they're likely to be all the happier.

Motivating girls to clutter clear has more to do with appealing to their sense of delight in collecting, sorting and displaying. Suggesting they find, look for, sort, match, clear and arrange will incite their curiosity and eagerness. Basically there is less of an issue about girls and clutter clearing (unless you're talking teens and bedrooms, which is a developmental stage and needs a different approach and another book). On the whole they seem happier to get involved and are able to both enjoy the task and see the long-term benefits. However, simply because girls are generally easier to win over and motivate should not let boys off the hook. Being organized and self-motivated is a necessary life skill. People who still expect their mum, wife or personal assistant to do their sorting and tidying for them are sadly lacking in personal responsibility and maturity. Boys *need* to know how to look after themselves as men, and womankind needs to back off and let them learn.

Participating in clutter clearing will also teach both sexes numerous transferable skills, including filtering, evaluating, making choices, breaking down a big job into several smaller jobs, recycling, reusing and thrift.

Participating in clutter clearing will also teach both sexes numerous transferable skills.

Differentiating between quality and quantity is a skill we could all benefit from revisiting time to time, as Constance Tyce, Early Years Advisor with Norfolk County Council, points out in *Communication Friendly Spaces* (Jarman, 2007):

> I recently visited a playgroup in a village hall. It was uncluttered on the ground but resources were easily accessible. The use of fewer high-quality resources is better than an abundance of second-rate equipment and clutter: I'd encourage everyone to have a clear out – hire a skip and throw out unnecessary resources, or sell ones and use the funds to purchase quality items.

Socially, clutter clearing will show children that we are all accountable for our own mess and that cleaners are not there simply to pick up after them. As Diane Reay, Professor of Education at Cambridge University, writes in her paper 'They Employ Cleaners to Do That' (1995), too many children and young people regard cleaning and tidying as 'not their job': the implication being that it is that of someone else; someone less important than them. Others simply don't know how to pull their weight or are just too lazy.

Clutter clearing will show children that we are all accountable for our own mess and that cleaners are not there simply to pick up after them.

Involving children in clearing and tidying will also contribute to children's spiritual awareness, honing their ability to know when and how to eliminate the unwanted in their surroundings and minds, and create environmental and physiological space in their life when they need it.

Make it into a project

Provide cameras for 'before' and 'after' photographs. Record the actual clutter clearing day too. Do a case study of one room and film the inhabitants tackling their clutter. Investigate vermin and bacteria. Hold a talk by your local rat catcher (with visuals). Find the dirtiest place in school – and the most fresh and clean. What is so bad or good about it? How could those good things be repeated around school? Interview representatives from all parties in school for their opinions on the following questions:

- What is clutter anyway?
- How do people feel when they are surrounded by clutter?
- What kind of clutter is there most of in school?
- How does clutter encourage dirt?
- What is your worst kind of dirt?
- Where is the dirtiest place you have ever been?
- Where is the cleanest place?
- How could we keep the school cleaner?
- Follow your rubbish. Create a provenance trail, i.e. classroom bins, school bins, rubbish truck – then what? Where does it all really end up?

Organizing this project falls under the remit of the communication members of the clutter clearing team (see Chapter 3).

Teaching staff

Our space is a reflection of our physiological health: it reflects how we are feeling inside. When we are happy and inspired, our surroundings tend to be clean and orderly, pleasant to be in. When we are miserable, the reverse is true – or it soon becomes that way. Cleanliness deteriorates, clutter accumulates and tiredness sets in.

Conversely, curiously, environment can affect us in the same way as we can affect it, although sometimes people have difficulty believing this to be so.

Ask most people what could be done to make them happier in their current job and after they have listed more money, more holiday and greater recognition, you will hear: 'I just want to be allowed to do my job better.'

What that final wish constitutes varies from person to person but their working environment very often has a lot to do with it. While new premises and even a whole new decor might be out of the question, many people will be happy with a good clear out and the opportunity to rethink the layout of their work setting. You can begin this with a clutter clear. A few people may need inducement, but most staff will be champing at the bit to do just this. The opportunity can lead to an explosion of inspiration and energy. All you need to do is release people to get on with it.

Three skins

In feng shui, the study of nature and the environment and the effects they have on the prosperity (health *and* wealth) of human beings at any given time and place, it is suggested that we have three 'skins':

- our epidermis
- our clothing
- our home.

Each or all of these 'skins' gives away our general state of physiological health at any particular time and you do not need to be a feng shui practitioner to be able to read the signs. We can all guess that a normally well-kept friend who lets her house go and turns up for an important meeting, unwashed and in dirty clothes is not feeling herself. What is particularly curious, however, is the way in which rectifying her space, i.e. clearing and cleaning the home, can have such a seemingly disproportionately positive effect on her appearance and subsequently on her emotional and mental health too.

School staff working with a colour therapist regularly spoke about keeping certain clothes only for school, citing the fact that they get dirty in school and the clothes had a 'school smell' that they could not seem to wash out. They were clearly unhappy about this; all of them wanted to wear what they felt were nicer, smarter clothes but did not want to invest in something that was likely to be spoiled in the surroundings they worked in. On the surface this might seem like a minor, even superficial, point, but clothing can make a tangible difference to the way we feel. Donning the same old dingy stuff day in, day out simply for practicality's sake can have a cumulatively grim effect upon people. Couple this with a similarly dingy school environment and add all the other professional concerns associated with the job, and the reasons for generic school malaise begin to seem clearer. Interestingly, one of the immediate effects people comment on after a clutter clear is how much better they feel the next day and often express this through their clothing by wearing a new dress or tie to match their fresher school setting.

Support staff

Administration staff frequently work out of some of the most cluttered spaces in a school. Usually it is the reception office where, jammed in between things to be collected and stuff just delivered, the photocopier and the filing cabinet, they can just about stretch their neck sufficiently to peer up and see who is waiting at the reception window. This is unacceptable for many reasons, the main one being that this important space has a powerful day-to-day impact on staff and children and is the first point of contact for newcomers and visitors to the school. Overly cluttered and disorganized, it will stress regular school users and plant seeds of doubt in the minds of people to whom the school might be 'selling' itself, e.g. new parents, potential governors and possible staff.

The reception and administration area should give solid messages of welcome, courtesy and competence. In many ways it is the hub of the whole school and should be experienced by all as well oiled and running smoothly. Sooner or later, if it is not, the wheel will indeed come off and run away with the organization of the whole school.

ACRAPULATE(TM)
a _ crap'_ u _ late – v.

1　To acquire or collect an array of items of little value.
2　To purchase quantities of items of only collectable value.
3　To purchase quantities of items and merchandise at prices below market value.
4　To hold or store items acquired through acrapulation.

As coined by Horist (2005) who also refers to collectors to as 'serial acquisitionists'.

Inducing the support staff to clear will depend on the most powerful personality in the office and how he or she is inclined toward clutter.

- Pack-Rat Paula will hoard for all she's worth keeping several copies of everything so she's never caught out and can always find what anyone wants at a moment's notice. Her office is stifling and leaves staff desperate to get out of it, with or without whatever they need.
- Bin-It-All Barbara can provide the same service but usually saves only

one copy of her work and that's often an electronic version. Her office is relatively spacious and as streamlined as she can make it. Staff usually do not even have to visit as she has organized herself to be able to respond quickly and electronically to most requests.

These two stereotypes are not dependent on age or length of tenure. This is a personality issue and the school would be better off with Barbara's methodology. While Paula does the job, she's also a fire hazard with a jumbo carbon footprint. She probably also has a heart of gold and the kids love her. She needs to clear up because, no doubt unbeknown to her, the way she works is causing huge amounts of stress for others in the same office and unnecessary frustration for those dependent on the efficiency of the whole admin service, not just Paula herself.

Gently revealing this to her should begin a journey culminating in a clearer office and more effective administration system or her redeployment to a place less damaging to the whole school. While the responsibility for this situation has to be shared, the solution can be dealt with promptly and impersonally under the auspice of a whole school clutter clear. The very idea will either rouse her out of her milieu or utterly defeat her, in which case other kindly and previously prepared measures can be implemented, i.e. moving her to another situation within the school or retraining her into a new role altogether.

Deconstructing office space

Break the administration and support office up as follows and deal with each area individually, allocating a certain amount of time to each:

- bookshelves
- noticeboards
- window sills
- coat racks
- filing cabinets
- cupboards
- desktops (including in-trays)
- desk drawers
- floor area, i.e. boxes and cartons.

Are things being stored for other people in this space? If so, why? Their stuff should be in their space, not yours.

Cleaning and maintenance staff

Cleaners, like teachers, take a pride in doing their job well. Their job, as the title suggests, is about cleaning as opposed to tidying up or picking up other people's mess. They should not need to clear things out of their way or they won't have time to clean properly, which is what they and everyone else want.

This seems to constitute a worldwide area of confusion, teachers are concerned about where their job leaves off and the cleaners' begins, pupils do not often even acknowledge that the role, or more importantly the people behind the brooms, even exist. Cleaners, caretakers, janitors can sometimes barely figure on their Richter scale of respect, which is a deplorable situation.

The comments on the left are indicative of the problems of cleaning in schools. We need committed cleaners, but the job seems to be getting increasingly difficult to fill and carry out. How can this change?

What cleaners want is simple: to be treated like people – by everyone in school including teaching staff and pupils – to be given the tools, time and access to do their job properly, and to be given the opportunity to be included in school initiatives. Cost cutting often reduces the amount of time in which they are allowed to clean a space and clutter inhibits them from getting at it quickly.

Clutter clearing cannot cure all of these issues but it can help cleaning staff move around classroom spaces more easily. They won't need much inducement to help with a whole school clear out and may have been muttering about it for years. Listen to what they have to say, as they will probably come up with some thoughtful and practical ideas.

This is not an 'us and them' situation. Cleaners also need to understand that classrooms are often shared and many of the people who use them are conscientious in their tidying, although others are not. Everyone benefits when there is respect and willingness, and everyone in school, including the children, should be working towards a cleaner, healthier and more sustainable environment.

A final word on day-to-day classroom rubbish; Bill Bryson says that while employing people or using volunteers to pick up litter is of course a good thing, what it can lead to is a situation where people, i.e. children, think that what you do with rubbish is put it down when it's finished with and that somehow, someone, somewhere will pick it up and take it away. This needs to be unlearned and fast.

Senior management teams (including headteachers and bursars)

Strategy is what it is all about at this level and what fills the hearts and minds of senior management teams, including heads, principles and bursars, is mostly money and results. That is what they are paid for. Sell clutter clearing to them via the financial benefits:

- Cheap continuing professional development (CPD) – a whole school clutter clear is team building; constructive, fun and extraordinarily cheap, compared with usual activities.
- Less expensive, less trouble and often as satisfying as redecoration.
- Creates a better looking product – easier to market the school to parents and pupils, easier to attract and retain good quality staff.
- Can lead to a pooling of resources and stop duplicative purchasing.
- Allows cleaners to clean more effectively and efficiently.
- Meets numerous government targets (see Table 1.1).
- Ultimately produces happier staff, leading to reduced absenteeism, greater retention, improved teaching, better learning and enhanced test results.

Hopefully, the school wellness strategy is subsumed by the accountants because well people equal increased standards, improved statistics and ultimately, a higher level of service all around.

Governors

What can governors do to help with clutter clearing? Ask them! For a start they might actually like to help out on the day. They might volunteer to do the tip run or oversee the skips or station the food trolleys (vital) or advise on reuse, recycling or saleability of the goods you recover during your clutter clear.

On the other hand they may not want to become practically involved at all and prefer to contribute later, perhaps working in partnership with one of the teaching staff and one of the cleaners to create or refine the Whole School Clutter Clearing Policy. Which they will definitely be able to see the point of as this will undoubtedly go down well with school inspectors; that and the clean and orderly state of the classrooms.

It would be respectful to alert the governors of your intentions even if you really only need their support in a consultative capacity. They should not need much convincing as to the usefulness of the enterprise and it will make them aware of your future intentions with regard to release of space, reduction of hoarding and emphasis on cleanliness.

Parents and PTA

Parents and the Parent–Teacher Association (PTA) are similar to governors in that they will not directly gain from a clutter clear in the way that staff and children will. None the less they will need to know about what you are planning and intending to implement, if only to be aware of new policy in terms of locker and desk clearances, lost property changes, zero litter tolerance (including food and gum), enhanced recycling, etc. Many will endorse all of this and some may actually be encouraged to volunteer as adult helpers or classroom assistants with specific clutter duties.

White elephant stockpiling for school fetes, summer socials, Christmas fairs, etc. should be dealt with in the same way as clutter throughout the rest of the school. These goods often spread and encroach insidiously. Storage for this type of thing needs to be thought through as carefully as any other area of the school. Generally it just accumulates without any initial sorting. Also, the person in charge of it is often over-protective of both the stuff and his or her role in looking after it, burrowing things away in the oddest places. He or she will often like clutter and feel resentful at being forced to rationalize it, but firmness must rein here as elsewhere. The school cannot become an extension of his or her home (for frequently his or her home is often full of stuff as well). There are other and more immediate ways to make money from good quality secondhand goods rather than storing them for a once a year blow out sale. Try eBay.

Other stakeholders (including further education)

Other people likely to be storing things at the school will be hobbyist and interest groups, probably with a long history of having used the premises (and who, endearingly to the school staff, sometimes come to see daytime users as the real intrusion in school, what with the kids and the noise and so on).

Further education, adult learning and community groups may also share the building. Routes to getting them to consider their goods and chattels include:

- Risk assessment – does the stuff have potential for causing an accident/incident in any way?
- Fire inspection – what would the fire officer say about the way things are being stored? Could there be any improvement?
- Health and safety – anything live lurking under their bits and pieces?

Shared premises can give rise to all sorts of misunderstandings but most people do see the sense in good quality storage pre-empted by a thorough clear out. Allowing them access and help with lifting and carrying may prove the incentive they need to join in your clutter clear. Often people just do not know what to do with their old tat so end up leaving it as it is. Providing the means for them to shift and finally remove it without asking them to share the cost might be just what gets them moving. Invite them to join you rather demand they conform, and see what happens.

Case study: the story of a school office

Two years ago Kim went to a seminar on wellbeing. One of the issues raised was the energy-sapping effect of clutter. As a result she returned to her large comprehensive school and immediately tidied her office. Twelve months later, however, she was in an even worse mess. Every bookshelf and cupboard was full; when her blue plastic boxes could hold no more so she resorted to cardboard boxes. They also quickly filled up and proceeded to take over all the available floor space. Her noticeboards were smothered with out-of-date memos and her desk with sticky notes. The in-tray was buried beneath a mound of government documents marked 'read and respond'. Although it was still possible to find somewhere to sit, even to hold a conversation with a colleague, it was becoming very difficult to concentrate surrounded by so much stuff.

Never the less, Kim thought she knew were everything was and anyway was far too busy to sort it out. Kim was in denial.

Interestingly, Kim's descent into chaos corresponded with her increasing preoccupation with being more efficient. As far as she was concerned, sorting everything out could wait until she was up-to-date with everything else and had the time. Despite 28 years of teaching and knowing that, in fact, the reverse was true – she would have more time and be more effective when, and only when, she had sorted her office out – she still clung to her guns. If only she could cram in more work and complete all her tasks she would then be able to tidy up!

By the end of term Kim was exhausted and overwhelmed by a sense of panic every time she entered her office. In her nightmares she was drowning in paper and dawn bought only more anxiety.

The final straw came as she stuck a series of notices onto her office window and noticed she was covering up the very view she moved into the room for. Entering the room brought a smile to her face and always elicited a positive comment from visitors. Floor to ceiling windows looked out to the left over a primary school playground filled with laughter. To the right she could see a beautiful old church. The view from cradle to grave was soothing and uplifting and she was covering it with memos about report writing and lost PE kit! For Kim it was a eureka moment.

She binned the memos and resolved to sort out the rest of the room. Two days of her holiday were spent surrounded by even more clutter as she ruthlessly shredded old documents, tossed out ancient video tapes and dying plants. She bought and labelled new files. She replaced and replenished plants and put up pictures of her children. She kept only the books that had meaning and replaced the utilitarian calendar with a feng shui version. She threw away sticky notes and filed government documents. At last her desk was clear. In celebration, she bought a new mug and a vase for fresh flowers and replaced her tired mouse mat with a new one emblazoned 'Keep Calm and Carry on'.

$\Rightarrow$

'How did I feel afterwards?' Kim answered in response to questions about the result of her hard work, 'I suppose as though I actually had time to think – that by clearing the space I was clearing my mind. It was a little like a meditation in that it (the clutter clearing) gives you energy and clarifies things. I was able to rethink priorities and settle to work rather than prevaricating.'

Six months later the clutter began to creep back, but today Kim is on top of the situation and tidies up before it gets any worse, also making time to buy flowers and water her plants. She even does her filing before starting work on the day's tasks. Her view is that all this keeps her sane and makes her an easier and more effective manager to work for. Everyone – family, school and of course Kim – benefits.

3

The run-up

Preparation, preparation, preparation.

- Starting out
- Create your clutter clearing team
- Leadership – your rallying cry
- Curriculum enhancement – clutter clearing's a life skill too!
- Planning and implementation – making it happen
- Communication – managing the message
- Training – more than 'sit by Nellie'
- Procurement and supplies – going shopping
- Hospitality – everybody happy?
- Sappers – the movers and shifters
- Disposal – going, going, gone

If you have clutter cleared before you will know how much it takes out of you on the day. Despite the final elation of a job well done when you have finished, the actual process is surprisingly emotive and physically draining. Paving the way for the day, enticing and accepting as much help as possible from friends, family and colleagues, ensuring everyone else knows what is going on and being practically ready will ensure that you can give full concentration to the job in hand when it is needed. Deciding upon and delegating pre-big-day tasks will help break the whole thing down into bite-size chunks and allow the clutter clearing team (with the support of senior management) to go into a pre-sales pitch guaranteed to build up enthusiasm in even the most hardened hoarder.

Starting out

At this stage you are talking in general terms about the idea of a clutter clear and are looking for volunteers to represent other users and contribute as key players within the clutter clearing team. Use this book as a blueprint for this hereafter if it suits the needs of the school. It will certainly save you re-creating the wheel. However, If you prefer to adapt these guidelines or would rather take a completely unique route, do so, but be aware that you will need more time to do this so start your planning earlier than is suggested here.

> I discovered myself getting rid of 20 years worth of resources because I knew I could find the same, if not better, stuff on the internet. (proteacher.net, 2008)

Create your clutter clearing team

Is there someone you know already to be an inveterate clutter clearer in your school? Does he or she have a good rapport with colleagues? Could he or she rally a team and build the momentum necessary to drive and induce the school into a massive clear out? If so you have the natural leader of your clutter clearing team. Or is all this going to fall on you, dear reader, if it's to get off the ground at all?

If you have time and are willing, fine. If not, share the job as fairly as possible and create a team comprising representatives from all user groups within your school, including pupils. This is about dialogue, not consultation; encourage everyone to be as fully involved as possible.

Roles needed within the team include:

- leadership
- curriculum enhancement
- planning and implementation
- communication
- training
- procurement and supplies
- hospitality
- engineering (sappers – the movers and shifters)
- disposal.

The number of people needed for each constituent role will vary according to the size of the school, but once the team is established, make the meeting an example of how the clutter clearing day itself will go. Let it be fun, productive and lively, and people will look forward to coming along and contributing.

Task each member of the team with a constituent part of the clutter clearing job and listen to what each one needs in terms of support. Much of this will be pre-empted in this book but allow people to individuate their task as much as possible to allow greater commitment. We all enjoy things more if we can have a say in how they are done. Make them all aware that this is not a one-off project, something that will be dropped next year in favour of the next 'big thing', and let them know too that the team is not simply being created for a one-off clutter clearing purge, but will become an on-going part of the school management structure. This is where clutter clearing in your school begins and continues, enshrined in school policy and established as part of school life, adhered to and respected for the enrichment and enhancement it brings to all.

De-cluttering has become a regular occurrence with the school having filled 14 skips in less than 12 months. (Shoot for the Moon Project, Dale Community Primary School and Creative Partnerships UK)

Leadership

Leaders must spell out quite clearly why it is worth everyone's while becoming whole heartedly involved in this clutter clear. Know why the school is doing it and show people what is in it for them. Give them the six good reasons if it helps. But also be sure of what *you* want from a clutter clear. Why it is worth the bother. How you visualize the school being once the clutter clear is complete. Articulate these things with confidence – and keep articulating them as people will need reminding when their spirits, quite naturally, flag from time to time.

Begin getting your Whole School Clutter Clearing Policy (see the example in the Appendix) ready for implementation immediately after clutter clearing day is over and in the interim look at how to make best use of cluttering clearing in your school to support various awards and accreditation schemes (see Table 1.1).

Curriculum enhancement

How does clutter clearing fit in with the requirements of the National Curriculum? What other work, particular to your school, is it supportive of? Clutter clearing is a relatively large undertaking, so advantage should be taken of it to wring as much as possible from the process to inform and support other work going on throughout the school. It seems a shame to waste so much time and preparation on a one-off chuck-out (your clutter clearing day), when it could be a useful journey that initiates a whole barrage of ideas.

Planning and implementation

Create your team towards the end of one term (winter is a good choice, as the next term, spring, is recognized as a good time for renewal and shedding of the old). At the beginning of the term you choose, announce a whole school clutter clearing day (CCD) to take place at the end of the same term, allowing plenty of time for everyone to get ready.

If the school is a large one and has not been tackled for years, a two-term run-up would be quite reasonable. However, do not leave so long between the initial announcement and final implementation that impetus evaporates. Careful timing is needed for preparation and enthusiasm to conspire to produce a successful event, which is why a broad timetable is needed. Many clutter clears flounder because things are not ready on the day. Planning and implementation are about overall management of the event: ensuring everything is in its place and ready for the identified date. When it is over, all unwanted goods should be off the premises, everything wanted should be properly stored, the school should be extra clean and the doors ready to open for business as normal when you all return to work.

Communication

Talk to everyone and keep talking. Remember, no involvement, no commitment.

Once a decision has been made to go ahead with a whole school clutter clear and the team has been recruited, proper dissemination throughout the school of the clutter clearing message should begin immediately to give people plenty of time to prepare. Everyone involved needs to know:

- What's happening: a whole school clutter clear is going to take place on [day and date].
- When: psychologically any kind of reincarnation appears to work best when started at the beginning of a new period of time (consider spring cleaning), so any of the following would be useful for a school clutter clear and revitalization: the first day of the season/term, or semester/month/working week.
- Where: be precise. Which areas of school are to be tackled? Only the classrooms/ lecture rooms and storage cupboards? Or are the admin areas, staffroom, toilets and public areas also included? How about the outside grounds and car park?
- Who's doing what: again, clarity is key. Let each person know what is expected of him or her. Which team he or she is part of; to whom he or she will report; who will report to him or her. Let people know which bodies are to be involved: is it simply the children and staff – and is that all the staff – or are parents, friends and family invited to join in? Also include a key contact for any immediate enquires on clutter clearing in general or about the day itself.
- How it will be done: refer to the role and responsibility of each member of the clutter clearing team, so people know who to go to with specific enquires. Tell them what will happen in the run up to the day and give a broad overview as to what will actually happen on the day, assuring them that a more detailed programme will be circulated closer to the day.
- Why: with any luck, 'why' will have been covered in any whole school staff training that has already taken place. If not, the reasoning behind the decision for this event needs to be made clear. Chapter 1 should give plenty of material for that.

A transparent approach is sensible, respectful and inclusive. On a practical level, everything lying around on the day will be fair game, and people will not want to lose things they value, so allow them the chance to put to one side what they really want to keep. Informing them up-front in this way will even encourage some to start sifting and beginning to get rid of stuff before the actual day. Circulate guidelines from the disposal team (see Chapter 3) so people can make an informed choice as to what to do with their unwanted stuff.

Some people will be a bit overawed by the idea of a gigantic sort out and won't know where to begin. Liaise with your training team to prepare everyone's thinking before the day by explaining the difference between clutter, storage and ornamentation (see following box). This often brings about an epiphany in the nervous and can dramatically ease the process of clutter clearing for them.

The difference between clutter, storage and ornamentation

Clutter is made up from things you cannot face sorting through. Clutter nags at the subconscious producing a distracting effect. Clutter by its nature is difficult to manage, ties down energy and is ultimately unhealthy.

Storage comprises clean, known, easily accessible items that have been previously sorted through and have a reason for being there.

Ornamentation is the beautification of a place. Do not throw away an object if it is truly inspirational or has wonderful memories. But remember, not everything can be categorized in this way. Be honest with yourself and select carefully (Purr, 2001).

Once your planning and implementation representative has disseminated to the team what is happening and when, you have to inform everyone else concerned with the school. Who, how, where and a bit more about what, can all be drip-fed nearer the date to keep interest high. For now give them what you have.

Letting people know

Marketing theory suggests that, in order to get a message across to as many people as possible, you need to use a *minimum* of three different mediums. In practice, and in schools, it should be about ten and it should be repeated at regular intervals (or people will forget).

In the meantime, for the sake of fairness, lucidity and potential success, the communication person needs to share (not tell) the information that there will be a clutter clear held in school very shortly and that everyone will be involved.

Here are some ways you can share this message:

- Posters – staffroom, staff toilets, staff entrance, reception, over the photocopiers, next to coffee points and drinks machines, above the kettle. Wherever the dinner or tuck shop queue congregates and parents gather.
- Email a clutter clear update – repeated once a week with new info added to keep interest fresh. Use quotes, humour, colour, different fonts, illustration – make it fun to look at, exciting to read.
- Tannoy – create a jingle, make it funny, tell them something new each time. Use thoughtful quotes and funny stories.
- Memoboards/flipcharts updates – specifically dedicated to clutter clearing day and strategically sited around school. Update regularly.
- Assembly – weekly countdown. Tell them what should have been done in the week gone by and what needs to be done in the coming week.
- Texts – one-line updates, keep them snappy and different; worth taking a peek at.
- School website – pop-up or banner. Both are annoying but could be justified in this case.
- Agendas – staff, governor, PTA, support groups, user groups, after-school clubs.
- Letters – can be time consuming and can add to the clutter, but it is a renewable, recyclable and powerful medium. (Paper may also be the most sustainable way of communication in the future; it is predicted that over half of the UK's energy requirements in the next ten years could be needed to drive PCs and laptops [BBC Radio, 2009].) It is also the most effective method to reach many people. Try to get everyone to sign for their copy and use a member of the clutter clearing team to act as postie, especially if you are in a big school.)

And some more esoteric but very effective means:

- Local radio announcement – your local radio station will probably do it for free and might like to interview you into the bargain. The children will love it.
- Local paper – as above.
- Printed balloons – (helium filled) little ones will get take the message home for the children, mums, dads, grandparents and carers.
- Badges – the bigger the better. Let the children design them.
- T-shirts – with day and date on. Clutter clearing team to wear them one week prior to the big day and can be used as cover-ups on clutter clearing day itself.
- Banners – over entrances and exits, inside and out.

What your message should say and how to say it

Respectfully contact everyone who may be concerned with the clutter clear even in the most tenuous way, informing them of the impending clutter clear. Request that they start to look carefully at things that could be considered clutter as on the day they will be asked to make a decision about whether they should stay or go.

Ask them to ensure that anything personal or professional that is extraneous to the school is removed from the school before clutter clearing day for the simple reason that it could otherwise be misconstrued as clutter and inadvertently discarded. This warning should be repeated at regular intervals using as many different means as possible.

Please note, 'extraneous' is a subjective term that will be interpreted differently by every school. How you arrive at your definition will be up to you, your team and everyone in school. 'The difference between clutter, storage and ornamentation' (see box on p. 47) will help you to decide, but things such as old fluffy slippers (in the staffroom), punctured and flattened footballs, buckets with holes in them, etc., should not be in doubt. This is real-life clutter and it's time it went.

Training

This about engaging people and ensuring everyone likely to be involved on the day of the clutter clearing has been prepared as best possible. It's so much more than 'sit by Nellie' (the traditional training fallback, based on the old factory system of inducting new starters by sitting them by an experienced older hand so they can watch and learn).

While this methodology still has its place, something less passive than watching someone else put rubbish into a bin bag is going to be needed to rouse serious interest in clutter clearing.

A whole school training event can do the trick. Focusing everybody on enhancing the school environment and held just before clutter clearing day, it is an undoubted luxury but one that often pays off by kick-starting the tardy and rallying the already enthusiastic for what is to come.

The following five sense audit and school user survey are just two ideas that could be incorporated into a day's training session.

Five sense audit

A whole school survey can begin things in quite a low-key although inclusive way. An audit of the buildings and grounds through the five senses is a straightforward, inexpensive and eye-opening (to use a visual expression) exercise that can really show up the best and worst in school environment in terms of sensory support. Various representatives of the school can be enlisted to help, including the children, who can actually be better at this than adults. A five sense audit works well as a simple walkabout exercise, although it may take some time as it is best not rushed. Deconstructing the school sense by sense may be unusual but it is worth taking note of these hidden persuaders as they are what influence people to buy in – or not – to your service, i.e. the school.

Normally, provided there is no disability or restriction, every person who uses or visits your school will be sensorially aware of every aspect of it as they make their way around the building and grounds. In an ideal world this will be a supportive, pleasurable experience but in reality is usually not. Clutter is not only something you trip over on the way in, it can affect more than one sense at the same time. For instance, if may not be only an eyesore (sight), it will often fester (smell) and can feel dirty (touch), sometimes constituting a physical health hazard in the bacteria it's supporting. Such sensory messages may occur intermittently or continuously but whenever they happen, it is a distraction for everyone (although it can be much worse for children). As Lorraine Maxwell (2007) points out, crowding and clutter can overwhelm the learning environment. She says, 'Some children have a harder time concentrating than others, and the more complex the environment, the more potential for distraction. It takes a great deal of mental energy to pay attention and when the physical environment is competing with reading or doing math it becomes more difficult to pay attention over a period of time.'

Teaching in a setting like this can be as equally debilitating as learning. The following description of a young woman doing her best to deliver her subject in unfavourable, although not particularly unusual, circumstances illustrates this.

Distractions

Although she couldn't see the cars through the vast, grimy classroom windows, Lorraine could hear them clearly as they whistled past on the road outside. She unwound her scarf, hot and starting to become bothered, but knew that opening the window would only increase the din and drown out everything being said. She was struggling to be heard as it was and continually raising her voice was beginning to wear her down. Blinds would have been of some help with the heat – had they worked and she been able to reduce the sun's glare – but as in the most of the rooms, several of them were broken, the others piled up in a dusty, jagged heap on the sill. She squinted and tried to focus on the washed-out PowerPoint® projection but found herself diverted by an ancient piece of display that flopped and bounced forward from its position next to the screen like a coiled spring about to take a tumble. She shifted her position, hoping for some relief but found her heel stuck to the floor with a blob of old, grey gum. Suddenly she felt overwhelmed. The door opened and a latecomer entered along with a foul and familiar waft from the boys' toilets. Had it always been this horrible, she wondered. Then she started to teach.

With all this to contend with it is a wonder anyone is able to teach or learn at Lorraine's school. Unfortunately this is not as extreme an example as it appears and Wollin and Montagne (1981) point out that the background of any interaction between a teacher and a student can have strong effect on the quality of that interaction. In school there can be several distractions affecting just one of the senses alone. Sometimes, for instance, traffic, lawn mowers, aircraft and internal noise can all be *heard* at once. This is auditory clutter, diverting everyone from the educational job in hand.

As you begin to tackle sensory clutter around your school, consider what can be done to remove, disguise or screen out such distractions. Additionally, notice what works to *support* each sense and note what could be done to develop and enhance this.

Five sense audit – whole school walkabout

See:

- Look for focal points whenever you enter a new space or cross a threshold. These should tell you immediately what this space is for and how users should conduct themselves. Any additional information should be clear and up-to-date.
- What can you see around you that distracts your learners from the message you want them to absorb? Take up their position in the classroom and look around. (Note that small children will be much closer to the floor and skirting board area and will notice things that are well beneath an adult's line of vision.) Does what they observe, including ceilings, walls, doors, windows, displays, storage, desk layouts and floors, support (or at least not distract) from the overt message you are trying to impart? If not, how can you make it so?
- What about you? Is there anything you can see beckoning you from your task, repeatedly pulling your senses in a certain direction?
- What do you see as you walk around school, as you walk out of school, as you walk into school across the car park, as you walk through the playground and perimeter of the grounds? Does it support the ethos of the school in every way? Does it feel harmonious? Does it make everybody concerned with the school feel proud, healthy and optimistic?
- How are staff facilities experienced? Is the staffroom welcoming and uplifting? How about the staff toilets?
- What do school neighbours and passers-by see as they look over the fence or walk or drive past? What kind of impression do they have of the school?

Hear:

- Apart from the noise described above (traffic, lawn mowers, aircraft, etc.) what other sounds are apparent in the classroom? Does internal noise, e.g. music, neighbouring carry-on or white noise, have an effect?
- Is music a regular feature of the school? If so, where about, what kind and how loud?
- Where are the loudest and quietest places in the school?
- How intrusive is the bell in you school? Would you miss it if it was not there?
- How much white noise, e.g. photocopier, computer, fax, land and mobile phone buzz, is there in the office, administration and reception areas of the school? Do people have to raise their voices above it to be heard? Does it intrude into conversations?

Touch:

- Floor surfaces can often inhibit or distract from work in hand. Slippery finishes cause people to pay attention to their feet in an attempt to avoid skidding and maintain balance. Uneven or broken finishes distract and break focus, as do torn carpets and cracked tiles.
- How densely packed are learning spaces, i.e. what is the footage allocated per occupant? Do people experience the footage as crowded?
- Do you have to check every chair before you sit down? Why? What is this like for pupils? How about table and desk surfaces (not to mention their undersides)? Worrying about what you are likely to come into contact with via touch can be both distracting and inhibiting. Minds should be free to concentrate on work rather than being endlessly pre-occupied as to what one might be leaning on or stepping in.
- How about keyboards and phones? These can cloy with stickiness and bacteria.
- Note the temperature in degrees as you make you way around the building. What is people's individual understanding (thermal comfort) of these spaces – do they find it chilly, too hot, clammy or dry?

Smell (and taste):

- The nose reconnoitres for the rest of the senses (Purr, 2001), which is not surprising when you consider, as Dr Charles Spence, a leading expert in experimental psychology of the senses at Oxford University and coiner of the term 'sensism', notes, that more of our genes are devoted to the detection of odours than to any other kind of sensory information.
- Ask what people most remember about school and they will very often recall the smell of the dinners – before, during and after lunch. Olfactory memory is longer lasting than any other. And the aroma of school food, particularly British school food, seems to be one of the most intense and long lasting sensory experiences most people ever encounter. In many old schools the smell is impregnated into the woodwork and is actually inescapable at any time of day or year. Fresh, it is not so bad; saturated into the floors and walls and mixed with cheap, equally pungent disinfectant, it is a powerfully unpleasant distraction that no one ever really seems to get used to. As a result, staff often complain that their clothes smell of 'school'. Children's uniforms can become the same by the end of the week. (Conversely, Monday-morning-clean clothes often fill the classroom with an overwhelming scent of washing powder.)

- Toilets can often be smelled from every entrance of the school. A terrible demoralizer for everyone, the stench is unhealthy on many levels and will insidiously undermine attempts to raise spirits and breed pride. In feng shui, lavatories are referred to as foul energy areas, for obvious reasons. Accordingly, where possible, they were traditionally placed well to the rear of a building, out of sight (and out of mind) and out of the nose's reach.
- Note also, the aroma of baking and coffee, and chemical smells from science labs.

Remember that, while you are carrying out this work, you show respect and interest for the people in your school simply by being seen to be collecting this information. Promises to meet *everyone's* specific and individual desires in this area will be unworkable, however. You are seeking the unifying factors or natural commonality that will ease and support the most important, fundamental needs of everyone.

Asking questions

Another means of generating thoughtfulness about, and build up to, clutter clearing day is through the use of questions which allow people to reflect on their attitude towards clutter and the spaces they work in. The following box shows a survey that can be used with all staff in school prior to or during a whole staff training day. At a training event people have the opportunity to get out of their usual cliques and work with other people around school (which often produces some unusual and thoughtful responses).

School user survey

Preparing for whole school clutter clearing

This a voluntary exercise for teams or individuals to complete prior to clutter clearing to start people thinking and talking about the clutter issues in their spaces and around the school. You might opt do this with teams. To obtain balanced feedback and interesting discussion, avoid natural cliques and instead create groups made up from a combination of all the various parties that use the school.

School user survey

1 What do you want from your space?

_____

2 What already works well in your space?

_____

3 How could you expand that (in your space or elsewhere around the school)?

_____

4 How could you personally help this to happen?

_____

5 What do you want more of in your space?

_____

6 What do you want less of in your space?

_____

7 What else do you want in your space?

_____

8 Where are your clutter 'hot-spots' (places where clutter tends to collect)?

_____

9 What are you currently gaining from your clutter – how is it benefiting you?

_____

10 Where is your clutter coming from?

_____

11 How can you cut off the flow of clutter?

_____

12 Who would you like to talk to about your clutter?

_____

13 What else do you need to do about your clutter?

_____

14 What will life be like when it is less cluttered (what will you have more/less of)?

_____

15 Are you ready to clutter clear?

_____

16 Any final thoughts or tips for others about clutter or clutter clearing (here or at home)?

_____

Visits

An educational visit by the rat man, otherwise known variously as pest control or sanitation, etc., is always entertaining for children, especially if his or her talk is accompanied by visuals and examples. Understanding what is potentially lurking in unlikely places around the school is thrilling for children and gives them an insight into why the school needs to clear out and keep on top of clutter and rubbish.

Subterfuge

Die-hard stock-pilers and the undecided can sometimes benefit from reading the author's book, *The Chattering House* (Anderson, 2007), an unassuming parable about the perils of clutter (apologies for the plug but I wrote it precisely for this purpose as I could find nothing else that would do the job). Leave it casually lying around for people to browse through when they have five minutes, as that is all it will take to read. If it makes them smile they will remember the common sense advice when clutter clearing day arrives.

Procurement and supplies

This is about having everything necessary to make clutter clearing day utterly successful. You do not want the whole thing to go array because the skips arrive two weeks late or because you run out of appropriate bin bags on the day. Everything that needs to be ordered should be thought about by the whole team and purchased via procurement as soon as possible after clutter clearing day has been announced. Once people have cleared they will often want to blitz-clean the space they have cleared and not wait for the cleaners to do it for them, so provide the tools and materials that they may do so. Your shopping list will vary according to your school's needs, and Chapter 4 includes ideas for team tool kits and repair kits that will probably be of use to most schools. Liaise particularly with hospitality team members as food and drink are imperative to keeping spirits up on the day. But think ahead and get everything well in time.

N.B. Procurement will also be responsible for the Stationery Amnesty the week before (see Chapter 4) and the pre-ordering of skips for the collection of rubbish on the day.

Hospitality

Hospitality is really about sustaining morale through the senses. An army marches on its stomach and so do clutter clearers. Sorting, sifting, shifting, cleaning: these can all become hard work very quickly if impetus is lost. People need to be repeatedly buoyed if clutter clearing day is to go to plan and ensuring as much physiological comfort as possible will go a long way towards meeting that goal.

Provide good quality and varied food throughout the day. Begin with a decent breakfast and keep it coming thereafter. If you can use the school kitchen, seriously consider asking someone to intermittently bake cakes during the day. The aroma of fresh baking lifts everyone's spirits exponentially and the finished products can be enjoyed by all, guilt-free in the knowledge that they will be able to work off the calories throughout the day. During the morning and afternoon deliver food and drink to clutter clearers. Circulate decorated trolleys around the school, with a hooter or bells. Let people know sustenance is on the way. Then gather everyone together for a fantastic party-style lunch at noon.

> The aroma of fresh baking lifts everyone's spirits exponentially and the finished products can be enjoyed by all, guilt-free in the knowledge that they will be able to work off the calories throughout the day.

Ensure music is playing everywhere and that it can be heard up and down the corridors. If you have a budding DJ, get him or her to create a few unique music-to-clear-to sets and distribute them around school on the day. Go even further and create a micro-team to deal specifically with sound around school, giving them the responsibility of ensuring that most musical tastes are catered for and that everyone can access what's happening. It could be a perfect task for a secondary pupil and a supporting role for primary children.

At the end of the day, people will probably be tired and may want to get away promptly. But do hold a final congratulatory 'closure' drink and nibbles. This will be a job well done, a team effort worth celebrating, so make sure you do just that and secure it in people's minds as not simply an extremely worthwhile effort, but as a day they thoroughly enjoyed into the bargain.

Engineers (sappers)

Need something put in place, taken away or even building? These are the people (a small team or unit) who you will be calling upon. Each should have their own pager, walkie-talkie or dedicated mobile phone, as they will be a kind of flying squad, constantly in demand on the day, and you won't want to be wasting time running around looking for them.

They will:

- decide where variously identified unwantables will go in the short term and how they will get there (enabling Disposal to sort out what happens to it thereafter)
- along with Disposal, identify deposit points, give everyone a floor map of the building and create appropriate signage so people know where they are on the day
- move stored goods and archive materials
- shift furniture (carefully and with health and safety in mind, arrange for any necessary lifting or moving equipment to be available on the day)
- dismantle and remove superfluous bits and pieces
- make up flat packs of new furniture that may have been ordered and to put in place once constructed
- rationalize (with other staff) the use of emerging space.

Again, their job could begin before the actual day. Respect their understanding of the school building and grounds and let them be the experts in this area. Ensure that they have trolleys and other necessary equipment to do the job properly and with minimal risk.

Disposal

Disposal is another key role. There is no point in clearing unless you know exactly how you are going to dispose of stuff and this is the job of Disposal. Prior to clutter clearing day they will need to identify drop-off points within school for each of the following:

- Reuse/redistribution – goods other people in school might be able to use. Or other people from other schools, clinics, surgeries, nurseries or hospitals. Give plenty of notice to potentially interested parties and hold a single day's viewing for them to check out the goods, then reduce what is left into the following categories and get it off the premises as soon as possible.

- Sell – e.g. eBay, assuming someone is willing to do the job and there is an identified place in which to store the stuff while it is being auctioned. You may earn a substantial sum of money for the school.
- Donate – bag and deliver directly to a local charity.
- Recycle – sort appropriately and either arrange for *immediate* collection or drive it away yourselves.
- Anything that can't be categorized as above – have skips ready and waiting. Three per small primary school is not unusual and it can rise to as many as 12 for a large secondary school.

Any or all of the above routes will enable people to more easily shed their clutter knowing that one way or another it will not be wasted.

Case study: it works every time

Dominic Mulcahy, headteacher of St John's Catholic Primary School in Manchester, has three leadership principles he puts into practice each time he takes up a new headship:

- Create a vision.
- Enable the right people.
- Invest in the environment.

As a repeatedly successful headteacher, he knows these simple values work. Testimony to this is the enthusiastic support he receives from teachers, parents, children and governors everywhere he goes. He is especially evangelistic about the power of place, believing it to be a huge underlying influence on the health and wellbeing of all school users although he rarely needs to spend a lot of money putting this into practice.

His strategy on taking up a new post is to involve the whole school in an enormous clear out and then to release people's inherent creativity to revitalize the school both inside and out. This will be done with a view to sensory coherence throughout the buildings and grounds: colours are themed and repeated – down to the last drawing pin – planting is appropriate and easily maintainable, and natural light is ensured wherever possible. The whole learning environment begins to blend and flow, allowing both pupils and staff to benefit from ease of movement and be uplifted by bright and cheerful decor wherever they go.

Tidiness is also encouraged and Dominic reiterates its importance each day during assembly when he urges children to, 'Look after each other, look after yourself and look after your school.' Emphasis is placed on maintenance and thrift.

To this end Dominic and his staff are aiming to reduce and eventually do away with lost property by instilling in pupils greater care for personal possessions.

As Dominic says, 'The school should be a haven, an oasis, an opportunity for children to experience beauty and dream of the person they can become.' Certainly Dominic's schools have been transformed and, in the transforming, seem to have transformed the transformers!

> *In 1998 Dominic Mulcahy took over as headteacher of St John Fisher and St Thomas More Catholic Primary School which was deemed to be in Special Measures with numerous key issues to be addressed. Within a year the school, situated in the most deprived ward in the UK, was removed from Special Measures and was described by Ofsted as '. . . the Rising Star of South Manchester . . .'. When Ofsted returned in 2007 ten original members of staff were still there from the period of Special Measures and the school was judged to be Outstanding in every category; an incredible transformation. Their Ofsted report stated: 'The Star has risen further and is shining brightly . . .'*

Let's do it! A checklist

Build up, show up

- A fortnight before
- A week to go
- Team toolkits

- Today's the day
- Eats time
- After lunch

- Closure

Who, what, when, where, why and how? Rudyard Kipling's six serving men cover everything you need to know about what will happen on CCD. Answer each of these one word questions (although not necessarily in this order) and everyone will know exactly what is expected from them and this is what follows in step-by-step plan for CCD. As you repeat the experience (although let us hope it will never be on the scale of this initial event), you will probably want to revise and modify the plan so that it serves you better each time you use it. It can then inform and support your own version of the Whole School Clutter Clearing Policy in the Appendix.

> I realized that after two years as a headteacher I had doubled the cupboard space in the school but still no one could find anything. A three week clear out began, which involved four skips and finds such as a dead mouse (flattened cartoon style), children's medicine from three years earlier and a book from 1958! However, the up was when we all came back after the summer holidays. All the resources were organized, we knew what we had, where to look and what to order. If standards rise this year I may attribute it to the marathon organization of resources – it is one of my biggest successes as a headteacher! (Alice Witherow, Headteacher, Benton Park Primary School)

A fortnight before

1   Decide: how will you know if your clutter clearing day has been a triumph? What are your success criteria? Use this for the basis of your evaluation (which you will want to carry out after the event to capture valuable feedback).

2   Issue a colourful, jokey reminder invitation to everyone you want to join in on the day (including cleaners, caretakers and janitors). Feature fun events of the day such as the fabulous lunch, daft team competitions and so on. Get people to RSVP to communications so you know who and how many to equip and cater for on the day. A note on safeguarding. Some invitees may need Criminal Records Bureau (CRB) clearance so allow yourself plenty of time to arrange this if it's necessary.

3   Begin clearing storage cupboards to create space in readiness for CCD. These spaces may need to be reallocated and should be empty to take the new, properly packed and easily identified goods. Alert building maintenance staff so they know how to deal with any resulting rubbish that arises.

4   Start working through lost property. Keep anything you can sell and ditch what you cannot via the usual routes.

5   Procurement team members should order rubbish skips in readiness (and to ensure their availability) for the day.

Dealing with display

Begin dismantling and sorting displays a good two weeks before CCD. Send unwanted children's work home with pupils and consider the options for staff-created pieces. Test how worthwhile it is keeping these things by scoring against the following criteria. Ask yourself, is each piece:

- current and accurate?
- appropriate and meaningful?
- effective and valuable as a learning tool?
- attractive or uplifting in itself?
- in sound condition (not curling, torn or yellowing)?
- annually useful, i.e. Christmas (and can be effectively stored when not in use)?
- of heritage value, i.e. manifests something interesting about the school's background?

If it doesn't work against at least two of the above, you know what to do. If it is unique, valuable or collectable but does not tick any of the above, sell it.

Photographing each display and archiving the results will result in a comprehensive and interesting record of display in the school and makes parting with it much easier.

6   Now move on to noticeboards. Remove ABSOLUTELY EVERYTHING that is not imperative and take a long look at what is left (too many Do This and Don't Do That signs can turn a school into a police station). If the board is empty, consider removing it completely – then and there – as left up it will encourage clutter on the wall. Give the resulting space a chance to grow on you rather than immediately putting something in its place and you may find the area pleasing left as it is.

Consider erecting a secure container in the school grounds to store wanted but not-in-use furniture. If you already have one and it is packed to the gunnels, make sure this is also sorted out on CCD.

7   If the Communication team members are recording the event for posterity, begin now. Involve pupils and make it a 'how to' project for other schools to learn from. Take 'before' and 'after' photos. Video everyone hard at work and interview them for comments throughout the run-up, on the day itself and on return to school.

It certainly was never planned – my room I mean. The whole environment just sort of crept up in there and embedded itself on the walls over the course of my tenure like the gradual build-up of algae in an aquarium. (Sullivan, 2004)

A week to go

1   Allow people to create themselves into faculty/department/subject teams linked to identified spaces – then give each team a name.
2   Brief the caretaker and cleaning staff (if they are not directly involved in CCD itself) so they know exactly what is happening and what is expected of them before, during and after the event.
3   Hold a Stationery Amnesty Day. Send manned trolleys up and down the school to collect unwanted pens, pencils, paper, etc.

4   Anyone with a locker might like to check it out. It may be a private area but these places do get a bit choked and the owner might like to tackle it.

All deposit points except the swap table must be removed by the end of CCD.

5   Pre-identify areas in the school for pooling certain types of resources and materials on the day. Sign the areas clearly and give everyone a floor map so they know where they are. Decide beforehand what's going to happen to these pooled goods during and at the end of the day.

6   Order food and drink for the day, once the number of people involved in the day has been ascertained.

7   Set up a staff swap table somewhere convenient for people to lay out anything they already know they want to part with. Allow passers-by to help themselves throughout the week and this will cut down the amount of stuff that has to be dealt with on CCD. Remember: one person's junk is another's crown jewels!

8   Identify deposit points around the school for use on CCD as below and give everyone a floor map so they know where they are:

- swap table – this stays in place for a week after the big day for anyone to help themselves from. Anything left thereafter is dismantled into the categories below
- sale point – anything that works and is clean could raise money for the school
- donation point – magazines, books and toys for hospitals, clinics, charity shops, etc.
- repair point – with work needed clearly identified for repairer
- recycle point – broken down into cardboard, paper, glass, etc.
- skip point – for anything that cannot be fitted into the above categories.
  Note: all deposit points except the swap table must be removed by the end of CCD.

9   Have plenty of lidded archive boxes ready for paper things that need to be stored long term. Label both the box and lid.

10 A repair kit per faculty/dept, including needle, thread, scissors, glue, string, cello/double-sided/parcel tape, screwdriver, hammer and pliers, will also be handy for immediate fixes.

11 See-through, stackable lidded storage boxes are the cleanest, strongest

and most practical way of storing goods in day-to-day use, so ensure these are ready too. Label both the box and lid.

12 A label machine per room or corridor will also very useful for creating good quality on-the-spot identification for boxes, files, etc.

13 Rationalize label font (e.g. Helvetica 12 point) and colour for use throughout school from the start. Storage is difficult enough to streamline without a complete mishmash of labels in different fonts and colours. Keep graphics clean and simple so people can ID goods quickly and easily.

Team toolkits

Compile a toolkit for each faculty/department comprising sufficient of each of the following for everyone:

- gloves (include some non-latex ones in case anyone has a latex allergy)
- aprons
- caps/hats (keeps hair clean and a faculty/ department badge can be pinned on the front – perhaps the children could make the badges)
- masks
- bin bags/recycling bags
- confidential waste bags
- brooms, brushes and microfibre dusters
- polish and cleaning wipes*
- antibacterial spray
- handwipes*
- kitchen towel
- you might like to include some handcream as a thoughtful gesture (dust and paper can be very drying).

*(If made from viscose or cotton, they are usually recyclable or compostable.)

14 Trolleys become invaluable throughout the day and there never seem to be enough. Have you a nearby supermarket that might support you by loaning you some of their shopping trolleys for the day?

15 Remember that communal spaces will also need teams, e.g. staffroom, hall, reception, corridors, etc., if they are not to be overlooked.

16 Turn the work into a competition – which team can fill the most bags/ finish first/create the tidiest cupboards or most space, etc. Have silly but relevant prizes ready in a lucky dip barrel, e.g. fancy frilly rubber gloves, posh room spray, fancy patterned dusters, etc. Winners to be announced at the end of the day.

17 Ensure that each participating person has a clearly named lidded storage box of their own in which to put their personal things for the day. It is

very easy to throw away things that should be kept – scarves, umbrellas, etc. – when things really get going. Once filled, stack these boxes somewhere safe for the duration.

18 Collect together enough radios, CD players to be able to play music everywhere throughout the day.

19 Ask each team to appoint a time-keeper to keep them on track for the day.

You're worth it

Holding a clutter clearing day at the end of term will make an unbelievable difference to the attitude of staff about returning to work the following term. A kind of vague excitement about the school being spacious, sweet-smelling and ordered will replace the usual indefinable creeping dread. In fact school becomes a place where people look forward to coming. Get to that point by starting with some decisions. Entice everyone to take a look at their things and ask themselves the following questions about each item. Then consider the advice that follows.

Q How often have I used this thing in the past 12 months?
A Less than three times and it's not earning its space – time to lose it.

Q Does it have an emotional hold over me?
A It might well do but it's holding you in the land of the past. Wave goodbye to nostalgia. Photograph it for posterity and move on. Let someone else enjoy it.

Q Does it just need fixing?
A Well, do it now or do not bother because you know it will never get done. Out it goes.

Q Could I borrow this if I need it in the future and get rid of my own?
A Yes. Good choice, you know what to do with yours – right now. No?
Are you sure …

Q Is there something better available on the internet or through other means?
A Probably, so get rid of it no matter how faithfully it has served you. Often you find what was useful once is no longer appropriate for what you need today.

Q But I'm looking after it …
A But why? Charge storage if this is really the case. Seriously, space is a rare and expensive commodity, do not give yours away easily.

$\Rightarrow$

Q What if I inherited it?

A People should think twice before leaving their stuff for someone else to sort out. Often done under the guise of 'It might be useful to the next person', it is actually a cop-out, a way of not facing-up to their own mess and leaving the clear out job for someone else. You are not a curator so you need have no issues about moving things along if you find someone else has left you a load of rubbish.

Q What if it is going to be worth something one day?

A It might be but do you have to take responsibility for it until then? Hand it over and let someone else sell it or sit on it.

Q Someone else might like it.

A Then put it on the swap table. If you know someone who might like it, attach a sticky note to the item with the person's name on it.

Q Why do I feel guilty about throwing things away like this?

A First, somewhere, somehow the things you throw away will be reused so you don't have to worry about that. Second, we all develop an attachment to the things we have around us; we become comfortable with them being there, even if (strangely) we don't like them. It is quite natural therefore to feel temporary discomfort when parted from these same things. Be brave and try to adopt an attitude of gratitude for the use you have had from these material goods rather than guilt at the thought of disposing of them. You will soon feel elated at the space and freedom you have created out of the chaos you have inhabited for so long.

Today's the day

1   If you get bogged down – ask for help! A second opinion or another pair of helping hands when you need them never goes amiss. Teacher and writer Shoshana Wolfe (2006) suggests you ask yourself this question each time you come across something that flummoxes you, 'When I find this next year, will I still want it?'

2   Identify up-front who gets what in terms of any newly excavated storage space around school and sign it accordingly so everyone knows what will live where in future.

3   Do as The National Trust do when clearing and cleaning, start at the top and work your way down, attic to cellar, ceiling to floor. Then work as nature does, from left to right, clockwise. This creates a kind of order and everyone knows what they are doing instead of just diving in anywhere.

4   Teachers' desks – clear, clean and then take a minute to ask yourself if you really need a desk at all. Could you release the space and use a dedicated,

secure shelf somewhere for all your materials? Might they actually be easier to store and access that way anyway?

The year I decided to get rid of my teacher's desk was a defining moment for me. When you think about it, what primary school teacher ever sits at his or her desk during the school day? My advice is to take a look around and see if you can live without that desk or table or rolling cart or bookshelf. It's likely that the extra space opened up will be well worth any inconvenience. Transitions (in this classroom) are smoother because there is more room to move around, clean-up is improved because materials are more clearly labelled and organized, and there is ample room in the various work areas for students to spread out. The physical environment is now roomy and uncluttered, welcoming and engaging. It is one in which our best learning can take place. (Robert, 2001)

Eats time

> Take a look around and see if you can live without that desk or table or rolling cart or bookshelf.

1   Pile high a couple of tea trolleys with drinks and lots of cake, croissants, Danish pastries and fruit – tempting food that looks and smells delicious (don't worry about the cals and carbs – they will be worked off during the day). Decorate with balloons, noisy horns and a warm smile, and circulate the school throughout the day. These comfort wagons will be a welcome break for all those getting their hands dirty. Their importance as a morale booster cannot be underestimated. When the trolley stops by it gives workers a chance to down tools for five minutes and enjoy a bite and a joke. Refreshed, they can set to again with renewed vigour.

2   Lay on an enticing and delicious lunch if you want people to remember this day with fondness (and create some discretional energy for the following term into the bargain). The importance of this midday break is on a par with the tea trolley. Food is a great social leveller and can contribute to an uplifting experience for all. Show people you care through the quality and quantity of food available. Anything left over won't be wasted as there is always someone willing to bag it up and take it home. Just be careful not to allow lunch to drag on too long or you will lose momentum for what is left of the day.

3   Ensure that water and other drinks are available throughout the day.

Decisions, decisions

Making a choice can be hard work sometimes. What to do? Not sure what to keep, so you keep everything just in case. Do you like to describe your eclectic hoarding as a 'lively learning environment'? Can't see what's wrong with being a pack rat anyway? If this sounds like you, you should also be able to hear the clutter bells sounding loud and clear.

But let's not get this out of proportion; untidiness, messiness even, is not a crime, and it is generally not an illness, although it can be desperately irritating and undermining. It is usually just a bad habit which is only a problem when it impinges upon the life you want to lead or of others around you. If, for instance, you are finding the quality of your teaching suffering because of the state of your surroundings or pupils are unable to move freely and safely around their settings, action is clearly required. Stuff needs to go.

Do not confuse de-cluttered with 'minimal' however. In this context de-cluttered is a physiological state, an all round release or freedom: the creation of a fresh palette. Minimalism, on the other hand, is an aesthetic, decorative choice. Once you have de-cluttered (emptied and ordered), thereafter you are at liberty to put back into that space whatever you want, at the pace you choose.

Understanding why decisions can seem so inexplicably difficult to make can allow people insight into why they occasionally drag their feet over clearing up and sorting out all sorts of issues in their life. Consider the word 'decide' itself. It means:

- to reach, make or come to a decision
- to make a choice or come to a conclusion
- to settle conclusively all debate or ambiguity
- to determine, settle, rule, conclude, resolve, opt.

From the Latin *decidere*, to cut off, decide. Connotations of: no going back. Finality.

A *decision* is the end of it (whatever 'it' may be). *Deciding*, though, is a process that leaves options open – sometimes so many options that a fug of matters, both physical (the things we surround ourselves with) and psychological (the issues that are going on in our head and heart) is created, continually creating a situation that is distracting and depleting.

'Deciding' can go on for years, leaving things open-ended and unfinished, 'just in case'. Afraid we might make the wrong decision and afraid of not be able to cope with the consequences, we can put off making a choice indefinitely. While this kind of behaviour is understandable in regard to life's big questions, e.g. to marry – or not, to invest all one's money – or not, it can become a life pattern spreading from Sunday supplement hoarding to hanging onto every piece of clothing ever owned.

To decide anything, we need the courage of our convictions: we must be brave, and be sure of our ability to survive the 'wrong' decision (should it be that). The

Harvard College Professor of Psychology, Daniel Gilbert, refers to this in his book *Stumbling on Happiness* (2006) as our physiological immune system: the innate ability within all of us to pick ourselves up when things go wrong and start all over again. It is there, we just have to believe in it; believe in ourselves. This needs confidence and when confidence is lacking all sorts of things slip including the decision-making process. But a slip is all it is. Do not allow a few weeks build-up of clutter to become an on-going habit. The longer it accumulates the more decisions you will have to make. So do it: decide now, and feel the weight lift from your shoulders.

After lunch

1   Anything that falls into the following categories which you decide you do not want, can be sold to raise money for school funds. Is it:

✓ interesting/curious/novel
✓ good quality
✓ little used or
✓ valuable? If so, get a price on it!

2   If you manage to empty a freestanding cupboard and have nothing to put back in it – do as you did with the noticeboards and seriously consider the necessity of actually keeping it. If you can part with it, do so and enjoy the space it releases.

3   Ensure all newly stored goods are raised off the ground to allow cleaners access beneath and prevent vermin setting up home.

4   When you are all done, create a storage and archive floor plan so everyone knows where everything is – and keep to it.

5   If building new storage shelving, affix the first shelf (the one closest the ground) a good 10–12 inches (30cm) off the ground for the same reasons as point 3.

Closure

1   If you still have a bell in school, this is the time to use it. Ring it one hour before the end of the day. When it goes, team leaders should ensure that everyone, including the head (who should be acting as an example in this), stops clearing and begins finishing up. Be ruthless at this point or the mess will drag on.

2   Clear, clean and store everything away.

3   One hour later the school should be in immaculate condition. THERE SHOULD BE NOTHING LEFT TO DO WHEN PEOPLE NEXT COME INTO SCHOOL. No jobs should be left nearly done or half finished, or this will defeat the point of the whole day.

> There should be nothing left to do when people next come into school.

4   Ring the bell for the end and meet at a prearranged place for a drink and wind down.

5   You will need this last get-together to formally close the day, but make it half an hour at the most. People will want to get away. Draw the competition prizes, toast the day with something fizzy and some choice nibbles. This has been a huge effort and it should be acknowledged.

6   Do not forget to collect clutter clear feedback – but keep it simple. The following brief questions should be sufficiently meaningful to capture people's thoughts and feelings about the whole process, and brief enough for them to complete before they leave:
   • What went well?
   • What did I learn?
   • What would I do differently next time?
   • Any other thoughts or feelings?

7   Remember, if people recall the day as an enjoyable event, they will be happy to participate again in the future, although hopefully that won't be necessary!

5

Re-creation

Really it's quite simple: clean, clear, enhance (aesthetics), energize; in that order. (Purr, 2001)

- Evaluation – did it work? How is it working?
- Teachers as placemakers
- Comfort learning
- Space by space
- Ask them what they want

If clutter clearing was the stage of editing and getting rid of things, re-creation is the design stage of the rationalization of your school. This is about carefully selecting what to put back or add into your spaces. Keep momentum going by identifying what has worked so far and building on it, gradually recreating each area of the school now it has been cleared. Simultaneously, begin a maintenance programme involving all users of the school to ensure a clutter clearing experience of the magnitude you have just been through need never be necessary again.

Evaluation – did it work? How is it working?

The clutter clearing event almost always becomes a kind of spontaneous team-building exercise. The laughing and exasperation implicit in the work required to clear a building of years of debris and waste create a kind of camaraderie that lasts long after the event. Frequently this is what people comment most positively on after the day. So, in retrospect:

- What went well?
- What was learned?
- What did people suggest could be done differently next time?
- What other thoughts or feelings did they have about clutter clearing or the day itself?

There is almost always good quality information of one type or another contained within these apparently innocuous questions. Clearing work of this kind often shifts thoughts and emotions, so asking for responses *immediately* following the event can capture fresh ideas and identify concerns previously unrealized or unspoken. Ultimately the feedback is as useful as the clutter clearing itself. What you do with it is up to you and your school, but colleagues will always be interested in the outcome of the evaluation, so do make your findings known.

Was it a success?

This of course depends on your initial criteria. What did you want from the experience? Many will simply have wanted to flush out their space while ensuring that if staff didn't enjoy it, they weren't exhausted by it either.

Education for All Operations is a UK social enterprise linked to the Education for All Trust (EfA). It takes unwanted learning resources, furniture and equipment from old schools, private offices and hospitals. In the initial three months of operation, EfA, working with the national schools' Private Finance Initiative (PFI; a way of financing new public sector buildings through commercial support) project in Bassetlaw, North Nottinghamshire, and supported by Transform Schools, (a school creation and maintenance company) successfully handled the first phase of a major new school build. They measure the success of projects such as this as follows:

- Four schools involved clearing 6,669 items (115.7 tonnes (T)).
- Diverted 109.26T from landfill (94.4 per cent).
- Re-distributed 4,072 good quality items (61.1 per cent) for reuse overseas.
- Dismantled and recycled 2,594 items (42T) through UK Environment Agency registered waste brokers and carriers to recycle: 23.2T of wood (into compost or energy recovery), 17.3T of mild steel metal, 1.5T of polypropylene plastic.
- EfA has also facilitated its first school partnership and teacher exchange between UK and South Africa.

- Four containers with over 2,900 items were sent to Cape College Education Office, Fort Beaufort, Eastern Cape, South Africa.

This is impressive. Your operation relative to this will also have been impressive. Ultimately the impact of your clutter clear will be educational, sociological, financial, ecological and more. The conclusions you reach as a result of this and the implications you derive from them will be unique to your school and worth sharing with others, as Education for All has done.

Teachers as placemakers

It is difficult, if not impossible, to separate (teachers') instructional activity from the physical environmental setting within which it occurs, say Lackney and Jacobs (2002). Yet while teachers attempt to create supportive learning environments and feel they do have some control over their working spaces, they often lack sufficient knowledge to enable them do so properly. Here again, researchers appear to have found that this whole area has been covered in insufficient depth during teacher training. Never the less, most teachers seem to know instinctively that the classroom plays a vitally important part in the work they do and that indeed they are the makers of a learning place. They understand, as Saeki (Saeki et al., 1995) wrote, that 'Learning in its broadest sense is a process of accessing culture via interaction with mediators in the surrounding environment: people, artefacts and *settings*' (author's emphasis).

While this book is primarily about the importance of clearing and cleaning the school, the following pointers about recreating and adapting learning spaces are included to help support the empirical understanding of setting that most teachers derive through their own efforts.

Unique selling point (USP)

'In designing spaces that re-culture schools, we want real cultures,' declared Francis Hunkins in his 'Reinventing Learning Spaces' speech for the American Center for Architecture and Education (1994). He continued, 'We want cultures that foster authentic activities as opposed to hybrid activities.' We still do.

He was urging his fellow architects to reconsider the whole idea of the learning space. But schools can do this for themselves by asking the same questions. How does your school foster authenticity and originality? What makes your school different? What distinguishes it from all the others in your neighbourhood? What are prospective parents, staff and community members moved by after visiting you? What do your staff and pupils bring with them each day that contributes to your school environment?

Whatever the answers to these questions are, they are your USPs – your unique selling point. They are what give your school strength, make it worth learning in, working for and being a part of.

A school, like a person, can often tick all the right boxes – clean, tidy, healthy, attractive, etc. – but ultimately lack that certain 'something'. That something is an extra depth of experience or personal style that gives a person or place, character, and makes being with them, or being there (in the case of a place), a more interesting experience. Of course displaying your individuality for others to notice in this way will mean you stand a risk of deterring one or two people who may not like what your school stands for, but your authenticity will at least be plain for all to see.

Apart from the physical structure and movement patterns around school that inevitably create a tangible identity, other variables also contribute. History, experience and values add to the patina of any environment and encourage in all users, especially children, a sense of their place in the scheme of things, of belonging. Displaying memorabilia in a new school which stands on the ground of an old one, for instance, supports continuity and recognizes the people who have been there before, both as pupils and staff. Likewise, prominently endorsing kindness and tenacity, honesty and bravery, and independent thinking as supreme accomplishments, equal in standing to good academic results and sporting excellence, will let everyone understand that your school places emphasis on developing well-adjusted, whole people rather than simply academic achievers or wannabe celebs.

Comfort learning

Logistics and comfort

Using the information collected during your five sense audit you should be able systematically to rectify most areas of the school in need of attention and enhance those where good things are already happening. As always, health and safety will be considered first but you should find that one of the natural results of a thorough clutter clear is a safer environment both in terms of physical environment and personal health.

Everyone will benefit from this because the place will feel better both kinaesthetically and for some reason, emotionally too. Build on this feel-good factor by adapting some of the tricks the retail and hospitality trades use to entice customers into shops and hotels. Bearing in mind how many schools are in competition with each for the same pupils and staff, it perhaps is something no school can afford not to do. Certainly making the place more pleasant for everyone isn't going to cause any harm and it may even contribute to higher standards for all.

Successful stores and hotels 'sell' their premises well before they sell their goods or services. The decor, fittings and fixtures, lighting, colour, scent and sound, and their staff, are carefully pitched and placed to attract the eye, ear and nose, to make you want to reach out and touch, to inch you over the threshold and keep you there. They know even if you do not buy the first time, if you liked what you experienced you will be back. Naturally their goods and services need to match the build-up or you'll become disillusioned and give up on them.

Can you see the analogy with school? Schools 'sell' learning, but, before that can happen, buyers (pupils) need to be enticed inside. But why reinvent the wheel when you are surrounded by good examples of successful selling? Take a trip to some of your favourite shops or hotels – cafés and pubs even – and learn from what they are doing right. Better still, ask them to come into your school and give you some tips. In the meantime here are a few to be going on with.

Light

Human beings constantly seek natural light because we function better in it, but it does need to be controlled. Ensure window dressings work both practically and aesthetically. Windows generally take up a huge amount of space and can become nothing more than a huge boring square of nothing on the wall when they are closed off with a blind or curtains. Whatever you use to cover the glass, it should add something to the general decor and ethos of the room and should not just act as a light filter.

Try to avoid long-term application of coloured film to the windows for the sake of data projection clarity. This is simply sacrificing nature to technology. Projection in full daylight should soon be available at an accessible cost and needs to be brought in as soon as possible if your rooms suffer from this problem.

If privacy is an issue, consider reverse blinds (rising from the sill upwards) or frosted film, which diffuses light, provides an attractive addition to the space and offers a little more seclusion.

Beware of other surfaces in your classroom. Opt for matt finishes or light will bounce all around the room causing visual difficulties for everyone. Conversely, if you have a darker room, reflective surfaces will aid what light there is to spread around the space. Remember that soft dappled light is wonderfully mellowing and, because it is constantly changing and often moving, provides interest in its own right too. Beware of fast-moving dappled light, however, as it can be distracting and difficult for people prone to epileptic fits.

Where possible, recognize the need for different kinds of lighting in any given space and provide both mood and task lighting for different types of learning and learners, using a combination of natural and artificial sources.

Future investment tip: natural overhead light from skylight-type windows is one of the most pleasant, natural ways of lighting an interior. Worth considering if and when finances allow.

Colour

Our responses to colour are both inherited and learned, and vary according to age, sex, climate, cultural and educational background and experience. Preferences and opinions on colour options are therefore likely to vary. If in doubt about what to chose, go to the colours of nature. They unite most people. Chambray blue works in almost all climates and from every light direction. It is the colour of the sky and, after all, most people like the sky. The same thinking applies to soft green (grass and trees) and turquoise (the sea, lakes, rivers).

Colour can also be used to delineate different areas, to stimulate or subdue, to expand or enfold space, as can light. When considering colour in your school and whether or not it is working, it can be helpful to take a photograph of an area. Enlarge it to A4 and turn it upside-down. Then, without trying to identify objects, simply notice the colours, where they are, whether they are varied or pretty much the same. How often are they repeated? Take everything into account: children's uniforms, landscape visible through the window, floor covering, bookshelves, etc.

How does this colourscape make you feel? What do you think about it? Is it cluttered with too much colour, or rather dull with a lot of repetition? We do not often deconstruct colour on its own in this way so this can be a useful technique for identifying where change might be helpful.

Scent

Odour awareness among children and young people is a growing trend. 'Scent-heads', as Avery Gilbert, author of *What the Nose Knows* (2008), calls this increasingly aroma-savvy generation, are even being catered for with their own aroma jockey, Odo7, a young Dutch artist who 'live-scents' clubs and music venues and synchronizes his sets to those of the DJ.

These children and young people are becoming as picky about the scents they wear, as the adults who generally fund their choices. Yet this smell awareness is still a distinctly personal and out-of-school experience except in the case of girls who individually perfume their clothes, hair and body as a kind of protection against the more lurid reeks experienced around the school premises – something like a nosegay that was used by the medieval population of London against the stinking streets (and people) of the city.

Once the smell-o-rama of the school has been mapped during the five sense audit, vile or peculiar smells can be targeted for future management as can uplifting scents (baking – if it happens in your school – cut grass from the field on a summer's day) for more widespread appreciation. Serious consideration could also be given to the creation of a whole new nasal happening for each space in the school building. There is experiential evidence to suggest that, as Charles and Ray Eames found in their olfactory multi-media performance in 1952 (Eames, 1952), strong images and/or verbal cues enable some people to experience the corresponding smell *of their own volition*.

Avery Gilbert (2008) also uses the term 'nasal persuasion' to refer to the way in which marketers have latched onto the potential for scent as another PWA messenger. Whether selling in this way is justified or not is a moot point but there is interesting research to show that feel-good scents such as biscuit and cake baking actually do cause people to feel good and act in a more helpful way towards others (Baron, 1997). This only seems to work, however, when the scent experienced is congruent with what is being experienced by the other senses, e.g. a zesty blast of grapefruit does not support the lulling auditory

Perception without awareness (PWA)

Involves:

- perception of a stimulus that takes place *outside of normal conscious attention* and remains unnoticed unless the individual actively tries to sense it (unlike subliminal perception which cannot usually be detected even when searched for)
- it can easily affect thoughts, feelings and, ultimately, behaviour.

experience of ambient, relaxing music. Grapefruit would in fact be better suited to a zippy, morning wake-up call, while lavender, matched with the ambient music, would create a more harmonious experience all around. But can schools learn from this? We encourage a greater sense of wellness via other sensory experiences so why not mood education by way of the nose too?

Whether you opt to go more deeply into the whole field of smell science or simply want to rid your school of the most pungent odours, the period following the clutter clear will be the most receptive in which to make your mark. As with all the other senses, do remember that, while each person experiences smell differently and may even be allergic to some, generally what works for most people in most circumstance, stems from nature at its most benign.

Nature

We gravitate towards nature. It is both a great leveller of people and the unifying factor between us all. Where you cannot let children experience nature directly, outside, bring it indoors (in a human-friendly and appropriate form, not as rats and spiders, bacteria, etc. – alright in their place but not next to us in the classroom). Use Table 5.1 as an at-a-glace guide to nature-profiling your school.

Display

Display is a never ending source of discussion for most teaching professionals and one that needs to take a look at itself afresh, along with the rest of the school.

So what precisely is the point of display? The answer will be different for everyone but it is worthwhile asking yourself this each time you are about to put something on show. What purpose will displaying this thing fulfil? For whom are you doing it? Do you ornament your own home, and if so why and with what? What criteria do you apply? And if you do put ornaments and artwork up in your own home, do you take the trouble to dust and polish them regularly? If the standards you apply at home cannot be maintained at school, perhaps the display in your classrooms should be reconsidered altogether.

'As I took down the old display,' said experienced teacher Gayle Robert (2001), 'leaving just those that were related to current studies, I immediately noticed a difference. The room felt less cluttered and students paid more attention to the displays that were left.' Yes, they would. Their environment has changed, becoming slightly more exotic and compelling. It's piqued their interest. Really, this is not hard to do. But display needs to be kept on top of, it is not to become tired and boring for everyone.

Display tips

- Keep display at children's eye level, or slightly above, but not below.
- Make sure all children's project work is displayed (not just the best).
- Properly credit children's work to each individual.
- Involve children in creating displays.
- Ask children to contribute questions with answers leading to pictures, writing and photographs.
- Minimize 2/3D displays including mobiles and other hanging paraphernalia. These were originally an arts and crafts device intended for intermittent impact. Today it has become ubiquitous and pervasive, cancelling out the impact it was intended to create and causing never-ending spatial and cleaning problems.
- Consider a wonder wall of things that children find fascinating and inspiring.
- In high traffic areas (entrances, corridors, dinner hall) host a past pupil's photo gallery featuring an ever-changing cross-section of different kinds of adult life from vets and parents to gardeners and carers, traffic wardens and doctors and factory workers. Ask each past pupil a few odd questions with answers likely to appeal to children, e.g. 'What was your best ever job? Why? What makes you happy? What is your favourite food/colour/ animal? Which sport were you best at?'
- Refresh the displays at the beginning of each term to maintain interest.
- Ensure all displays are current, relevant and properly looked after.

Also ask yourself these questions:
- What are your reasons for creating a display?
- How will it support learning in a particular environment?
- Is display the best way of doing this?
- Is it as attractive as you can make it?
- Is it in line with the values of the school?

$\Rightarrow$

Signage

Well thought out, good quality signage demonstrates respect for proper communication, both for school users and visitors, and allows the school to get value messages across in an explicit way. In general it provides four main functions:

- direction, e.g. way markers
- information, e.g. posters, bulletin boards, notices, brochure racks
- identification, e.g. rooms, equipment
- safety, e.g. hazards, fire exits.

First-rate signage is an opportunity to make a good first impression on those new to the premises. On the other hand, confusing, obsolete or hard to find information will lead them to question the whole enterprise (see www.Planeta. com). When signage works well it can also be a chance to promote goodwill among regular users as a courtesy that keeps them up-to-date and suitably informed of school business.

Not to abide by all of the above will place many people, particularly those with visual difficulties, at a disadvantage or in an 'information deficit' situation.

Monitoring signage is an important on-going task that very often falls between two stools resulting in an unmonitored, dated mishmash of mess throughout the entire school. This is tantamount to allowing randomly chosen people to roam the building with key messages, stopping now and then to impart a bit of information then passing the rest of it on later when it's out of date.

Signage is simply static information. It should be as helpful, inclusive and relevant as possible to all school users. Informational notices should change fairly frequently to renew potential interest in regular readers.

Compulsion notices can build up very quickly especially around entrances. Avoid too many finger-wagging (Stop *This*, Do Not Do *That*) signs or the place can end up overly regimented and may inadvertently implant ideas into readers' minds. Instead revise your

Good signage is:

- clear
- concise
- accurate
- consistent
- placed where people are looking (or feeling for in the case of Braille)
- securely mounted
- non-reflective but well-lit
- in a colour and texture contrast to its background
- in a plain font (no italics or serifs).

walls regularly and tell people what you do want from them (Do *This*, Do *That*). And don't forget good manners – Do This, Thank you (thereby making the positive assumption that *of course* the request will be complied with).

Noise and acoustics

It is not just pupils who suffer from cluttered auditory settings. Kimberly Kopko (2008) commenting in her paper on the work of Dr Gary Evans (Evans, 1992), an environmental and developmental psychologist, points out that teachers in noisy schools are more fatigued, annoyed and less patient than teachers in quieter schools. They also lose instruction time due to noise distractions and have a compromised teaching style.

Teachers in noisy schools are more fatigued, annoyed and less patient than teachers in quieter schools.

The following ideas may help decrease teacher voice strain and increase children's hearing, comprehension and appreciation for silence and more subdued noise:

- internal ambient sounds may help counteract external din as the ear tends to focus on these first. Try rustling leaves or bamboo, tumbling water, birdsong, etc.
- ventilation and heating noise – reduce whenever possible
- white noise – switch off, e.g., projector, computer, etc., when not in use
- creeping habituation to high noise levels can be slowed by making regular volume adjustments to AV and PA equipment
- contrast day-to-day racket by introducing 'down sound' spaces, e.g. forest glades, still or slow water, the library, church or museum
- ear plugs can produce a new sensory experience – quiet! Let pupils try them out
- create a make-shift sound box around the teacher: an actual boxed area with hard, reflective surfaces beside and above the normal teaching position to help with voice projection
- fit a voice transmission sound field system in the classroom or throughout the school if funds run to it. This can be installed in a day and allows teaching staff, through the use of discrete microphones, to preserve their voice and speak at normal conversation volume. In turn, this has a powerfully calming effect on the children, who are generally used to being shouted at all day and tend to respond by upping their own volume
- rubber, carpet and cork flooring minimize footfall noise and muffle furniture scraping
- hessian or felt as backing mount on back wall display boards helps minimize echo

- teach delayed verbal gratification and respect for quiet with a timed hush period. Relieve the strain with a bust of laughter to signal the end
- tai chi and other martial arts rely on silent concentration – some children may enjoy the challenge – try mime for those who prefer something different.

Energize

Once a space has been cleared, cleaned and arranged to your satisfaction, you can begin to bring in things to dynamize the space and its users. This involves the placement of living things and/or artificial objects depicting the kind of mood you would like to create. Plants and flowers; pets and fish; water features; lava lamps; rocking chairs; depictions of movement, e.g. paintings of kites in flight, children playing, yachts under sail; fans (or open a window for a fresh breeze); plasma screens – all will work. Chose the kind of energy you would like the room to foster and hone the space accordingly. Lastly, don't forget people. Rooms which are barely used tend to feel fusty and unloved. Make sure everywhere in the school is visited and occupied from time to time to avoid this kind of cheerless atmosphere building up.

Density and crowdedness

Lorraine Maxwell, Cornell University, suggests that square footage per child (density) in the classroom is as significant to children's academic performance and interpersonal relationships as the number of students in the classroom. High density comes about as a result of less room per child, not necessarily more students. Careful space planning can make the most of tight areas as the great architects Charles Rennie Mackintosh and Antonio Gaudi knew. They understood what was needed in terms of sociopetal space (space that draws people together) and sociofugal space (space that repels people from each other) and created their buildings accordingly. They also knew that the arrangement of space is as significant as the quantity.

Crowdedness is a personal perception of space which, of course, is very difficult to cater for where a number of people are involved, as each person's idea of what is enough will be different. Never the less, it should be acknowledged. Animals go mad when they are cooped up, as do we, although too much space is as alienating and almost as debilitating as too little. There are generic spatial distances and arrangements that seem to suit most cultures fairly well. The enduring popularity of Mackintosh's tearooms in Glasgow and the semi-circular parapets of Gaudi's Parc Guell in Barcelona are worth studying in

Proximics

Anthropologist Edward T. Hall (1963) formed the term 'proximics' as a means of describing set, or consistently measurable distances between people as they interact. Body spacing and posture, according to Professor Hall, are unintentional reactions to sensory fluctuations or shifts, such as subtle changes in the sound and pitch of a person's voice. Comfortable personal distances also depend on culture, social situation, gender and individual preference. In the West, overcrowding in school classrooms or corridors can unintentionally disrespect these distances and result in misunderstanding and animosity between pupils who feel they are constantly in each others' 'face'. Intermittently allowing them space to spread out and breathe can ease the situation temporarily but long-term alleviation can only be brought about by allowing a comfortable amount of space per pupil.

this respect and can provide huge inspiration for smaller spaces in schools.

Storage

The rather unglamorous and often frustrating question of storage can become – or remain – a needless bone of contention if it is not sorted out straight after CCD. Many people find the whole thing a bore and frankly it *is* hard work trying to find somewhere appropriate to store everything in our space-starved Western hemisphere. Yet the peace and relief that come from finding something first time and knowing exactly where it can be stashed for safekeeping really are worth the initial bother of identifying storage space. As Kristy Acevedo (2008) says, organization is not necessarily about neatness; organization is about automatic preparedness for all tasks.

It is also true that everything you have, you have to look after. Everything you own needs maintenance. The more you own, the more of your life you spend looking after things rather than living. This is worth remembering as you start sorting for storage. How much of your life do you want to allocate to looking after your stuff both at work and at home? While there is undoubtedly a percentage of materials that is core to the needs of your work in school, there will probably also be an amount that is discretionary, i.e. the deciding factor in whether it is necessary or not is yours, no one else's. So, precisely how much you burden yourself with is up to you.

> Everything you own needs maintenance. The more you own, the more of your life you spend looking after things rather than living.

To have and to look after

Several years ago I stayed in the wonderful 29 Palms Inn on the edge of Joshua Tree National Park in California. As part of the unusual service they offer there, a fascinating talk about the natural history and archaeology of the area is held every Saturday morning. During the talk I attended, the speaker showed us a rusty old lidded tobacco tin which, she said, was an artefact that had been found in the desert and had probably been used by the local native people. They would have chanced across it themselves in the first instance and prized it as a small but useful ready-made container. She went on to explain that the Native Americans here were travellers and that their containers were usually self-made from clay, leather or straw as pots, pouches or baskets respectively. She also pointed out that, as nomads who did not settle anywhere for long, everything these people owned would have had to be carried with them, or dragged by horses. In this situation too many possessions quickly become burdensome so they were careful about what they accumulated. In contrast, she asked to us to consider how many containers we owned; how many drawers we had in our homes, how many pockets holding bits and pieces in our clothes. In my case, I realized, it was plenty and all holding plenty of stuff. Stuff I wasn't sure I actually needed . . .

Dawna Walter in her seminal book on storage, *Organised Living* (Walter and Chislett, 2001), advises, 'Learn how to access the space you have; how to prioritise what you need from it; and how to manipulate it to fit your needs.' She continues, 'Good design is not an extra, it is the root of living well.' She is writing here about the home but her words are applicable to all built environments, especially schools.

When seeking new or more appropriate areas for storage other than the usual cupboards and cabinets, consider the following:

- dead space – under stairs, behind doors
- overlooked and under-ultilized areas, overhead (think Delft rack and mezzanine platform) and beneath eye level
- consider vertical not just horizontal space – build up, as well as along or beside
- storage should be streamlined; integrated or built-in where possible
- where it cannot be integrated, make a feature out of it and coordinate, colour- and design-wise to work with the rest of the room
- display open and accessible goods in such a way as to whet the curiosity – check out the retail sector for tips where 'selling' in this way has become an art form

- responsible centralized storage of core materials avoids individual harbouring and repeat purchases, promotes conservation, is easier to sort for currency and frees-up actual learning space
- metal cupboards for paper – keep vermin out and contents dry
- children and adults should have a secure and clearly identified place in which to store their personal possessions – promotes peace of mind and personal responsibility
- photograph children's work, store virtually or make individual hard copy portfolios, and then send the actual work home
- use coloured guttering secured horizontally in rows along a single wall as a stable but flexible means of holding frequently changing displays. It works particularly well with face-out books.

Visit other very different places from school and notice how they store and organize – spas, museums, factories, hospitals, gyms, etc. can be a mine of fresh ideas that can be used in school. Remember, properly organized storage will support lesson 'flow' by eliminating unnecessary queuing time and allowing work to begin promptly. Streamline this arrangement still further by repeating stores of highly used replenishable materials such as paper, glue, etc. in several key areas around the room. Finally, take the advice of Winnie the Pooh when he says, 'Organising is what you do before you do something, so that when you do it, it is not all mixed-up'.

Use coloured guttering secured horizontally in rows along a single wall as a stable but flexible means of holding frequently changing displays. It works particularly well with face-out books.

Table 5.1 shows an at-a-glance check for the balance of your school environment.

Table 5.1 Harmony table

CONTRAST	FRESH	SPACIOUS
Neither too stimulating nor too relaxing	Air moves and is refreshed regularly	Very little stuff or clutter anywhere
CURRENT	TENDED	VITAL
Display and notices are supportive and up-to-date	Building and objects respected by all	Is alive, vivid, growing, uplifting, light-filled
NATURAL	CLEAN	APPROPRIATE
Both natural and artificial textures and finishes	Tidy, allowing access on top of, underneath, inside of anything	Everything fit for purpose, including clothing

Space by space

The threshold

The purpose of any space should be apparent immediately upon entering it. Whenever you open a door, step through a gate, draw back a curtain, or simply move from one demarked area into another, you are entering a new threshold and should be able to tell what happens in this place and have the opportunity to adjust your behaviour accordingly. This is particularly important at building entrances. These areas are crossed repeatedly during the course of a normal school day and have the potential to repeat a message several times over to the people using them. This is a great uplifting opportunity if the message is a thoughtful one, congruent with the school's ethos; but can have the opposite effect if it is a depressing, retrospective tale about the state of the toilets or what everyone had for lunch yesterday. Combine that with smeared glass doors, a tatty old bulletin board and curling display and you have missed a chance for raising morale and restating sound values.

Your school should have what estate agents refer to as 'drive-by' appeal.

Main entrance – external approach

Your school should have what estate agents refer to as 'drive-by' appeal. This simply means your establishment should look from the outside like it means business and knows what it stands for. Rightly or wrongly, judgement will be made fleetingly as potential parents, governors, staff and children cruise by your school on the way to somewhere else. Impress or reassure them by ensuring the following guidelines are adhered to:

- school sign: should be highly visible, immaculate
- gates: make sure they are working/tidy/open fully
- path: clean, in good repair, attractive
- plants: keep them LIVE and weed-free or remove them altogether. Yellow/red flowers and shrubs are most uplifting
- car park/parking: where possible make it subordinate to building
- building's windows: these are the eyes of the school – should be sparkling, clear, sticker free
- doorbell/intercom is the voice of the school and first point of contact with the public; it should be working, audible, hospitable

- general signage: keep it minimal, polite and positively framed
- front door: should be in good state of repair, opening fully, isn't blocked by piles of stuff behind it
- outside lighting: should work and be sufficient and fit for purpose.

Main entrance – internal

The most important space in any location, the entrance or entrances, are crossed and re-crossed repeatedly throughout the school day, creating an imprint on the user each time. This can be a good or bad thing depending on the quality of that experience. Make sure it's a supportive, revitalizing and inspiring one by carrying out regular checks:

- lighting: working (no dud or flickering bulbs) functional, glare-free
- corners and skirting boards: visible (creates impression of expanding space), clean, unscuffed
- decor: light, airy, nature referenced, appropriate
- artefacts: relevant, uplifting, good quality, inclusive
- stability: solid, dry floor, fixed matting will create under-foot stability
- scent: hint of cleanliness. The school SHOULD NOT suggest toilets, sweat or old food. Nor nasty air freshener. Fresh air/flowers are good, as are beeswax polish and natural, good quality oils
- sound: ambient, relaxed but not silent
- signage: few in number, positive in pitch, courteous in wording, current in content. Awards and other recognitions are good.

Headteacher, bursar or principal's office

This room is about leadership. As such it should be representative of the whole school in its ethos, design and upkeep. Floor to ceiling paper stacks with chairs squeezed in-between will not do. The first impression upon entering this space, the office of the head of the organization, should be one of welcome, confidence, business-like preparedness and inspiration. Remember the headteacher is filling a role and that role is one of direction and responsibility. People will expect these qualities when they enter this office and will be uneasy if they do not find them. Reassure them by putting the following measures in place:

- site the office to the fore of school not hidden away at the back, as if hiding
- demark space within the office. Allow curved area/low seating for informal chats; angled worktop with upright chairs for more official conversations

- privacy: office should be restricted entry, secure. It should not be used as a thoroughfare to somewhere else by all and sundry
- storage will be integrated and rationalized, clutter-free, tidy, thereby creating a spacious feel around the office itself.

Likeable libraries

- Well over half potential child borrowers are browsers who come to the library without a book title in mind.
- Covers sell books (so display them face-out with their colourful covers rather than spines on show).
- Books displayed near the circulation desk are always more popular.
- Many children will want to borrow a book they have 'tasted' beforehand, i.e. have had read out loud to them.
- Eye-level positioning sells books best (bottom shelf is worst, top shelf nearly as bad) to everyone.
- Cosy reading corners work, encouraging children to settle in and read.
- Silence can be intimidating, but a subdued level of chat is appropriate and achievable.
- Change thinking about library design from 'warehouse to workshop' (Gary Natriello, Library Director) better fits the needs of older digital-savvy students.

Classrooms

Reams have been written about classroom design and there is plenty of good research available. The following points are intended for no more than quick reference but do, as Judith Heerwagen says in *Biophilic Design* (Heerwagen et al., 2008), recreate for the senses as well as the body:

- streamline: light and colour, sound, textures and materials (too many different surfaces in a space cause tactile clutter and confusion)
- contrast: while an excess of stimulus will cause overload, too much sameness will send children to sleep. An *occasional* touch of discord will provide the necessary jolt to keep them alert
- furniture and storage: size it right: pretty obvious but sitting on the wrong size seat all day can be exhausting. Try it and find out for yourself
- ensure children have sufficient space to work without banging elbows. Allow for lefthanders when planning your space as they often get forgotten

- keep overhead and ceiling space relatively free of bunting, mobiles, washing lines, etc. or it simply gets choked with swaying paraphernalia
- learning/activity centres and information stations: keep them mobile and streamlined (allowing cleaners access behind). Rolling cubby units can be good for this
- create a variety of microenvironments within a single area by informally demarking different learning spaces with low dividers or screens, a change of flooring, or wall colour or simply stripes on the floor
- audio visual: keep distracting display and furniture well away from the edges of interactive whiteboards
- storage: if they can't reach it, they won't use it. Make it pupil friendly
- soft furnishings: cushions, beanbags, rugs – great if you can clean them otherwise, watch out for the lice!
- factor-in flexibility: can things be fairly easily changed by you and others? But don't change things too often as children need time to acclimatize and an excess of adjustment can breed agitation. Promote socialization if you want to by moving children not furniture
- privacy: make allowances for those in need of quiet and solitude. Create alcoves for children to retreat into
- ensure there is sufficient space for children to move freely. Remove obstructions, create clear pathways. In these over-indulgent times any additional exercise a class gets will only do them good
- minimize muck: place a doormat just inside or outside the classroom doors to limit dirt carried in on shoes
- bins: use D-shaped bins; raise up off the floor and attach to the wall at wrist height, encouraging people to deposit rubbish in them as they enter and leave and making access easier for cleaners. Make them colour coded and you'll include some recycling education into the bargain
- regularly rationalize student furniture. Removing just one desk or table can make a huge difference to a classroom
- desks can be a distraction for some pupils. Take the advise of educator Beth Lewis and try turning the desk around so the closed end is facing the pupil and he or she can't reach inside to mess with clutter
- age appropriateness: children's needs change as they age. Rooms need to adapt around them, e.g. teens need to learn more about adult behaviour and expectations than toddlers
- avoid over-personalizing a classroom to your particular taste. Others may have to teach, and certainly many children will have to learn, in this same space and may not share your love of cushions and stuffed animals or a café atmosphere (kettle, coffee, mini-fridge, etc.). Remember, if in doubt, turn to nature. Most people flourish in a welcoming, clean, light, sweet-smelling and spacious setting. Save aesthetic

peccadilloes for your home, the ideal outlet for individual decorative expression

- temperature and comfort: people experience temperature differently. A layered school clothing policy allows individuals to remove items when they are hot and still be acceptably dressed. Allow for this *inside* classrooms by offering streamlined, fold-back wall hooks (which also ticks health and safety boxes by avoiding the usual tripping and skidding as clothes slip off chair backs onto the floor). Remember, thermal discomfort is a sensory distraction that undermines children's concentration and learning.

Teacher desks

Do you need that desk – or not? Exactly what function does it fulfil? Consider exchanging it for a storage cart or trolley, or even a couple of shelves with some coordinated filing where you can safely store your bits and pieces. Some teachers find this an extremely freeing experience both in terms of the space it releases and in the personal physical mobility it allows them. Others take re-creation as an opportunity to try re-positioning their desk: moving it around their teaching space to get a feel for what works best for everyone. With or without your desk, always ensure you site yourself so you have full view of the classroom with no one behind you; where you have good eye contact with pupils; can hear what is going on; and can move fairly nimbly to where you need to be, should give any teacher a subtle but powerful authority in his or her classroom.

Future investment: if doors in your school open into the room, re-hang them so they swing to the wall instead. This will probably involve a rewire to accommodate new light switch placement. (Take the opportunity to drop it to a more ergonomically appropriate wrist level so children and the disabled can reach it too.) Better still, fit sliding pocket doors which tuck away into the wall and create a wonderful feeling of 'flow' throughout the school as doors seem to disappear altogether.

More future investment: replace all cornered or angled furniture with curved versions. Ovals, circles and kidney shapes allow greater ease of movement and create a much more comfortable atmosphere. Think about standing desks too: small round raised tables of the type found in bars and bistros, where children who move a lot can work more freely and contentedly. According to scholastic.com, about 75 per cent of the total body weight is supported on only four square inches of bone when humans sit up straight on a hard chair, so it is not surprising children wriggle as much as they do to relieve the pressure on their backsides.

Support offices

Highly visible, usually extremely busy, and a fount of information and support for all, the admin and support office is more likely to attract clutter than anywhere else in the school. Yet for it to function properly it needs to maintain clarity and collectedness, acting as a standard the rest of the school should be aspiring to:

- first impression: calm, ordered, respected, friendly
- demarcation: decide exactly what happens in here – reception, switchboard, lost property and archive storage, word-processing, parcel drop-off/collection, etc. Should/can any of these be done elsewhere, releasing this area to become more streamlined and creating a more organized and serene atmosphere both for users and visitors?

Corridors

How many times a day do you frequent the corridors? How about pupils? They have a similar effect on users in terms of repeated exposure as entrances. Put this high usage to good effect by using the corridors as another learning experience for pupils. Before displaying materials, however, get the basics right or your good intentions will be wasted. Ensure that floors are solid, stable, subdued and clean. Rubber works well. Superior quality carpet and underlay is easier for cleaners to maintain, muffles noise better and lasts longer. Lighting should be full-spectrum where possible (mirroring the effect of sunlight) and glare-free. Wall mounted up-lighters are a good idea if the ceiling is low, as these create an impression of height. Keep decor appropriate, i.e. calm greens and blues, for encouraging hushed movement around school and make sure furniture is tidy, well kempt and ergonomically designed for best traffic flow. Finally add a display, keeping it current, uplifting and meaningful.

Staffroom

Many schools consider themselves lucky to have a staffroom at all never mind one that actually nourishes the people using the facility. But if such a space is available, surely it makes sense to extract the best use possible from it? Following clutter clearing, users might like to take the following into account:

- atmosphere: think soothing, warm, welcoming, rejuvenating
- entry policy: who, when, why – inclusive and as welcoming as possible
- room name – is 'staffroom' a suitable term anymore? If not then what?

- function: is the room for rest or work? Both are not a good idea. Preparation and marking need a dedicated setting of their own
- layout: avoid the retirement home look (chairs lined up around the perimeter of the room). Bistro area for eating combined with alcoves and 'snugs' for more reflective moments can work well
- decor: think longevity, durability, nature, relaxation, spaciousness
- kitchen/cooking area: cared for, clean, committed to (discourage plastic food container build-up)
- furniture: combination for upright eating and laidback comfort.

Hall/refectory/gym

This kind of multi-usage is not ideal but is becoming increasingly common as a result of new-build finance and footprint restrictions. However, eating, exercising and assembly are completely different school events demanding different kinds of environment. After all, who wants to partake of a meal in the middle of the local gym? Or settle down to yoga on a damp floor between the odd squashed pea and scent of gravy? And how much gravitas and pride does a hall impregnated with a combination of sweat and school dinners carry?

If you are faced with this rather unsatisfactory situation, make the best of it by keeping the area as scrupulously clean as possible. Keep the space clear of all associations of other uses during the task in hand, e.g. ensure mats, balls and gym equipment are put away during eating periods and that the place has been thoroughly aired before being used as a gym. Extractors should be used to help clear the atmosphere after all usages. Keep displays neutral and flush to the walls.

Toilets

Project CLEAN, the USA service dedicated to safety, cleanliness and hygiene in public school restrooms estimates that, for various reasons, approximately 40 per cent of middle and high school pupils in America avoid using the toilet while at school because of their negative atmosphere. National USA hero Bathroom Man, otherwise known as Tom Keating, began drawing attention to this area of neglect and abuse in 1996 and has not stopped campaigning for better sanitary conditions for pupils all over the world since. His agenda for change includes tried and tested methodologies focusing on pupil accountability, increased janitorial awareness and greater respect for the issue as a whole in terms of initial restroom design and construction (for more about Tom Keating and his work see: www.failuremag.com/index.php/feature/article/mr.clean).

In the UK, Bog Standard, a campaign based on the research of Sue Vernon and others in the University of Newcastle upon Tyne (Vernon, 2006) found that, 'Going to the toilet is more than just a physical reflex. The whole ambience must be comfortable and relaxing.' Key findings also uncovered that avoiding going to the toilet can increase the risk of health problems such as urinary tract infections, constipation and incontinence in children. And that, 'More than half the boys and one third of the girls avoided using the toilets throughout the day to defecate, blaming dirty toilets, inadequate privacy, and fear of intimidation and bullying.' Their report says anecdotal evidence from health specialists in other European countries suggests that this is a problem affecting the entire continent. Of course this is appalling and it will take more than a clutter clear to put the situation right. Never the less, 'many a mickle makes a muckle' as they say in Scotland. Start small as Bathroom Man did. Clean and clear and encourage the following actions. Future investment might allow you to consider the wider recommendations of both Project CLEAN and Bog Standard, and move closer towards making this human necessity as straightforward and stress-free as possible for everyone.

Mixed gender toilets are NOT conducive to privacy and security for either sex or any age.

- safety: toilets should be bully-free, properly hygienic (make sure surfaces around cubicle locks are cleaned every day)
- sensitivity: mixed gender toilets are NOT conducive to privacy and security for either sex or any age. Architects may encourage them on the grounds of space-saving (read money saving) but going to the toilet in a safe, private setting is a basic human necessity recognized by the most materially poor of societies, even where formal built facilities may not be available. Ignoring this is to encourage a lifetime of health problems for children and young people
- access: full entry during breaks
- condition: toilet paper and antibacterial gel always provided, lockable cubicles (with lock in working order).

Interestingly, it took legislation to ensure school restrooms were kept up to standard in one American state where the State Senator, Kevin Murray, observed, 'We have requirements for bathrooms for prisoners, for farm workers, for restaurants. The amazing thing is we do not have any state requirements for bathrooms in schools' (for more about Senator Kevin Murray's work on school bathrooms (*Oakland Tribune*, 2003). Cleanliness and order for this basic human need shouldn't have to be a legal requirement anywhere. Regular maintenance and respectful usage should see to that.

Outside

Worthy of a book in itself, outside school space is frequently just another dumping ground, ill-considered design-wise and vastly underutilized as a learning area. In many cases teachers and children cannot even look out over it from the classroom as it is blocked by over-zealous displays or blackout blinds which are kept shut most of the time due to the problems with IT projection.

Often the only piece of 'green' in the neighbourhood – if the school is lucky enough to have a field – and sometimes the most valuable piece of property in the area, this space should earn its keep. Devote another period of time to dealing with the outside as a separate area. Clear it as systematically as you have done the interior of the school, then re-create it taking into account awnings and canopies to shade window areas, and provide shelter for outside teaching and play. Think about square-foot vegetable gardening for the children, a contemplation garden incorporating the safe use of water, a wildlife meadow and sensory spaces for all school users to enjoy throughout the school day and over the seasons.

Ask them what they want

Almost 20 years ago, Dr Anne Taylor, founder and programme director of the US Architecture and Children Institute in New Mexico, offered suggestions for enhanced learning environments. They were based on workshops and seminars where teachers and children were asked to redesign their classrooms for the future. Here is a representation of those ideas:

1 Eliminate desks and substitute other personal space storage and writing surfaces.
2 Design light and moveable partitions. Children will be moving through the environment in the future.
3 Create mobile furniture that has multiple uses for children.
4 Create an environment that is receptive to new technology and electronic devices.
5 Create stackable seating scaled to children.
6 Provide for privacy in the classroom. Corners are relatively unused spaces which could be privacy 'relief' places. Some children learn better by themselves or in small groups in private spaces.
7 Use innovative storage systems for tables and computers to free space for other activities.
8 Give heating, cooling and plumbing information in the architecture by leaving a portion exposed for children to learn from.
9 Design colourful, attractive and hospitable hallways.
10 Design a Velcro wall to which special instructional items can be attached.
11 Design hallway graphics and mini-museum (Taylor, 1991).

When was the last time you canvassed this kind of opinion in your school?

6 Keep going. Keep growing!

We were born to unite with our fellow men, and to join in community with the human race. (Cicero)

- Hearts and minds
- The wider picture

Many people find the whole clutter clearing and rationalization process a bore and sometimes it is difficult trying to find somewhere suitable to store everything in our space-starved hemisphere. Yet the satisfaction and relief that come from finding something first time and knowing exactly where it can be put away for safekeeping really are worth the initial bother. You cannot do it on your own however; anymore than you can single-handedly implement sustainability in school or responsible procurement and waste management practices. If children and young people are to crystallize into responsible citizens with an inherent interest in maintaining the world around them, respect for the school and the wider environment beyond need to be factored into the curriculum. In many places this is already being done. This chapter is simply about turning up the emphasis. Remember, as the author Joan Welsh once famously advised, 'If you're coasting, you're either losing momentum or else you're headed downhill.'

Hearts and minds

So the big day has been and gone. Things are pretty much back to normal except that now everyone's enjoying a cleaner, brighter, fresher workplace and learning environment. But how do you keep it that way? How do you stop clutter-creep starting up again? Now is the time to grasp the still-enthusiastic moment and let zeal lead the way. Clutterlessness is a strange thing to be passionate about but once savoured it can become an obsession. Do not allow it to become crushed under the weight of day-to-day school life. Factor-in maintenance. Think ahead, as they say, do not let day-to-day operations drive out planning.

School management and teachers

Maintain staff momentum by keeping up the fun factor and by making their job easier through the implementation of a Whole School Clutter Clearing Policy (see p. 104).

Enhance relations between cleaning staff and teaching staff by enabling each to better understand the expectations of the other, e.g. do cleaners want chairs up or down when they come in to clean the room? Do teachers have time to pick up rubbish during the day? Assumptions never work and simply lead to frustration all round. Increased insight into what each party needs should allow higher and more consistent standards of cleanliness and hygiene in school.

Meet our cleaner

Place a photo of the class cleaner on the wall to fully integrate cleaning staff into school life (if he or she is comfortable with this). Allow children to make personal contact with cleaning/maintenance/janitorial/custodial staff so they are less some faceless person who clears up after them, and more someone the children know and say hello to every day and want to help with their work.

Junk that mail

Open your mail over the recycling bin each morning and stop yourself squirrelling work away for later. Dump it there and then so you are not delaying decision making. Commit yourself to dealing with the saved stuff by the end of the day and you will keep on top of paper.

Clutter Café

Clutter Café is an informal interest group. Make it realistic and not simply another burdensome commitment by scheduling it in just monthly or even bi-monthly. Liven it up by including a more personal aspect from time to time: swish (swap and trade) parties for clothes, gardening (seeds and plants), household items, etc.

Throw ten things

Throw ten things is an exercise to be done on a regular basis, whisking through your space and bagging ten things you do not need. Seal the bag and pass it on to someone else for recycling or disposal so you are not tempted to look inside and save it all at the last minute.

Study and research

Why not encourage reflective study of the effects of clutter clearing on children's learning among staff as work towards a higher qualification? This kind of thing makes ideal material for teacher status credits and higher degree modules, and the work can only contribute to a field where little solid, long-term research is currently available. We *know* cleaner schools work more effectively. Others need proof and you are in a position to provide it.

Teacher gifts

Isn't it about time this often embarrassing and usually wasteful end-of-term/semester ritual was reconsidered? It puts terrible pressure on less financially able parents and creates a pile of things most teachers do not know what to do with after the initial moment of gratitude has passed. Why not replace it with a whole new approach based on found or made objects only, things that can be consumed, recycled or returned to nature quickly, cost little and involve children in making a more personalized gesture. Examples could include a feather, leaf, flower (not wild or from someone's garden), pebble, poem, story, painting or photo, even something baked or brewed.

Tots

What is in it for little ones in terms of tidiness? How to get them involved? Keep the whole thing simple and easily remembered so it becomes routine. Tidying should become expected behaviour, an integral part of an ordered day allowing a sense of security and independence to develop. Be specific in your tidy requests. Incentives can work but should not become the norm. Contain their play or they'll simply move into the next free space and clutter that too. Allow sufficient time for tidying and let them finish, do not do it for them. Help tidy time along by:

- changing the learning state with your voice and body language or music when it is time to tidy. In Japan, space-use is used to communicate a message to children by changing the atmosphere (Itoh, 2001). Tots should approach quiet areas and take up their tidy task or area of responsibility (allocated or drawn from a lucky dip on a weekly basis). This can be done in partnership, teams or as peer coaching, i.e. a reception child alongside a nursery child

- making it fun and a tidy tots' game so they will be more likely to join in; try 'Mystery Mess' – a sticker for the person who finds the paper clip or sweet wrapper, etc. and tidies it away. Or 'Robots', everyone moving in a mechanical way
- making it more competitive – who finished first, who tidied most, etc.? try tidying to 'Flight of the Bumble Bee'; tidy up should be finished by the end of the piece.
- Change music each term to prevent habituation (see www.preschooleducation.com/scleanup for a wonderful array of songs) or let children bring in their own music
- racing against an egg timer
- remember some tots will need to be taught to tidy as they simply won't have had any prior experience of what it means. You may need to be quite precise about what is required from them.

Children

Clutterbusters' Club: introduce a monthly meeting following the staff Clutter Café. It should include the previous month's feedback and round-up, quizzes, games and practical make-it-from-junk activities (see *Making Mad Machines – Why Throw It Away?* by Jen Green [1992]). Also include a regular clutter think-tank. Revolve clutter busting duties, badging-up individuals or teams as:

- building and grounds assistant (litter grabbers, hard hats and clipboards are always popular)
- noticeboard and display monitor – assists with creation of new designs
- storage and supply attendant – tracks, sorts, collates, puts away, replenishes as necessary
- wildlife supervisor – looks after plants and pets
- flying squad (with proper kit – aprons, gloves, etc. – and walkie-talkie) – deals with non-dangerous ad hoc accidents such as spills and drops
- entrance inspector – specifically ensures that all access/egress points, including the main

Ready-made tidiness

Check out *Tidiness: a teaching resource* (see www.ccc.govt.nz/learning/education resources/citizenshipgovernance) for a view as to how other people have integrated clutter clearing thinking into the curriculum.

See the website www.citizen.org.uk/education/sen/word/environment.doc for a special needs resource intended to assist children with learning difficulties to understand more about their immediate and wider environment and what they can do to help improve it.

Tidy the Classroom at www.learning.luton.gov.uk is a virtual tidy game aimed at foundation stage children, which may support those in need of more help.

school entrance, are in tiptop condition. Uses a checklist (virtual- or paper-based) to record condition of signs, paintwork, cleanliness and tidiness, proper functioning of gates, doors, etc., and reports to a member of staff.

Each job should have a log book into which observations and incidents are included before it is passed on to the next person or team holding the role. Over the course of a year this will make interesting reading and extracts can be used on the school website as a blog.

Teens

Encourage students to maintain desks and lockers in a state of orderly cleanliness by factoring-in a ten minute clear-up during which teachers are seen to be carrying out the same task. Introducing a competitive element (cleanest classroom?) and encouraging peer support and pressure can make the process more interesting for them.

Create an Eco Committee or Envirominders group and let the members organize a school litter pick. Increasingly common and valuable as a community unifier, this type of event takes everyone in school outside into streets, parks, the beach, riverside, canals, residential homes, etc. to pick up litter within a half mile radius of their school. Rubbish bags, gloves, litter grabbers and high visibility vests are usually available from local environmental services for the day and the media enjoy the opportunity to shower praise.

Most nations now have their own versions of the Keep Your Country Tidy campaign. Along with the other initiatives detailed in Chapter 1 (Table 1.1), they offer young people the opportunity to become involved in local, national and global environmental movements as they chose. These can be grandiose political activities, old-fashioned nature conservation or local clean-up schemes intended to benefit the immediate community. Whatever they opt

> ### Girl/boy tidy tips
>
> Girl/boy preferences are obviously clichéd but work in many instances. Do remember to allow flexibility within the suggestions and let children who would rather tidy differently do so. In the end it doesn't matter as long as they get the job done.
>
> - Boy preferences – make it a physical exercise: jump over, crawl under, lug this, reach up for that, look at me, I'm a team member. Rotate leadership fairly, show consistency.
> - Girls preferences – sort, order, straighten-up, group, make neat, work together. Allow autonomy and creativity in tasks.

for they will be better informed and more capable of contributing to the world around them because of skills they have learned at school. As Margaret Mead anthropologist and writer said in 1944, 'Never doubt that a small, group of thoughtful, committed citizens can change the world. Indeed, it is the only thing that ever has' (for more about Margaret Mead see: www.interculturalstudies. org/main.html).

Children, as with the rest of us, are not apart from nature; they are a *part* of nature. This is their world: they need to know how to respect it and look after it and not expect someone to come around with a big brush and clean up after them their whole lives.

Learning bonus across the age groups

Clearing, tidying and conservation teaches and encourages:

- enhanced hand/eye coordination
- movement and exercise
- decision making
- self regulation/personal accountability for own mess
- reward and consequence understanding – no story/playtime until rooms tidied
- inclusiveness and team membership – everyone has to muck in for all to benefit
- delayed gratification – a sense of accomplishment and increased self-esteem (pride in a job well done)
- patience and empathy for others – slower class members need support and encouragement from peers
- resilience and endurance – having to do something (possibly) perceived as a bore, unfair, a waste of time, etc. Not being able to do purely what one wants to all the time
- thrift and appreciation of things both natural and manufactured.

The wider picture

Reduce; reuse; recycle; recover before disposal. This kind of thinking is only going to increase in the coming years. Wastefulness has apparently had its day. If prudence is not taught at home it will be instilled by the state through the school system. Whether this is right or wrong is neither here nor there; it is happening now and is probably a natural response to the excesses of the recent past. Our environmental and philosophical carelessness has been unbecoming and could well be our undoing as a civilization. But make do and mend needn't be all hair shirt and knit-your-own-muesli. Thrift is fun and does lead to real innovation. The old adage about adversity being the mother of invention is true. Too much freedom (money and stuff, power without responsibility) can lead to lazy thinking and emotional discontent. Eventually, getting what you want too regularly becomes unfulfilling and unhealthy. In the West we have generations of young people who, for various reasons, have never experienced the pleasure that comes from making a sustained effort at something you enjoy and have an aptitude for.

Earning your way, making your own individual contribution, be it growing vegetables, sewing curtains, writing letters, sweeping the streets, organizing events, coping with emergencies or listening to others in a way no one else can, enables people to feel needed, useful and deserving of the wages and peace of mind that come with service. The root of the word 'earn' is harvest. But it is impossible to harvest without sowing first. And when you understand firsthand the endeavour that has gone into making, growing and tending things, you are much less likely to be careless with them or disparaging of them. An appreciation of provenance, the previous route of things to the point where we find them in front of us, brings about a natural marvelling and integral respect for the world. And surely that is one of the most fundamental gifts we can pass on through education to our children.

Whole School Clutter Clearing Policy

Introduction

This school has completed and benefited from a whole school clutter clear involving all school users and intends, forthwith, to maintain a clear, clean and orderly school environment to enhance the lives of those working and learning in it.

Our pledge:

We (children and staff) will do this by:

- ✓ thinking before accumulating

- ✓ disposing of things no longer needed in a prompt, safe, respectful and sustainable manner

- ✓ clearing and tidying regularly:
  - ✓ at the end of each lesson
  - ✓ at the end of the day
  - ✓ at the end of the week
  - ✓ once a term

- ✓ maintaining individual and community storage areas to the highest standards

- ✓ integrating as many aspects of clutter clearing as possible into the curriculum and extra-curricula activities

- ✓ holding a community litter pick once a year

- ✓ encouraging contribution and involvement with regard to clutter clearing from everyone concerned with the school

- ✓ monitoring and evaluating our clutter clearing effectiveness on an annual basis

- ✓ be a best practice clutter clearing school example and support to other schools and organizations interested in our whole school clutter clearing work.

Note: the above Whole School Clutter Clearing Policy is intended as guide only. You may wish to create something completely different for your school and that is, of course, fine. The more personal it is to your school, the more meaningful it will be to all within it. However, do ensure it is read and understood by everyone, including the children. Make regular reference to it; enlarge and laminate it and display it prominently (but not so prominently it constitutes clutter!) around school for everyone to see. Update it as you go along so it always remains relevant and current.

References

Acevedo, K. (2008) 'Managing Private Teacher Spaces: seven personal teacher areas that need organizing', available online from: www.classroomorganization.suite101.com/article.cfm/classroom_organization_topic

Anderson, J. (2007) *The Chattering House*, available online from: http://workininginwellness@gmail.com

Barnett, C.L. (2006) 'Could Your Classroom be Making You Sick?' available online from: www.tandt news.com/archives/2006/Sept06/CouldYourClass.php

Baron, R. (1997) 'The Sweet Smell of Helping: effects of pleasant ambient fragance on prosocial behaviour in shopping malls', *Personality and Social Psychology Bulletin*, Vol. 23, 498–503

BBC Radio (2009) 'Virtual Warming, Costing the Earth', April

Bryson, B. (2009) Notes from Bill Bryson, available online from: www.cpre.org.uk/campaigns/stop-the-drop/litter-and-fly-tipping/litter-notes-bill-bryson

Caine, R. and Caine, G. (1997) *Unleashing the Power of Perceptual Change: the promise of brain based teaching*, ASCD

Clark, R.C. (2002) 'The New ISD: Applying Cognitive Strategies to Instructional Design. *Performance Improvement*, Vol. 41, No. 7, 8–14

Cohen, P. (2004) 'Spaces for Social Study', *New York Times*, 1 August

De Botton, A. (2007) *The Architecture of Happiness*, Penguin

Design Council (2005) *Learning Environments Campaign Prospectus*, available online from: www.designcouncil.org.uk

Eames, C. (1952) 'Bread' is a series of panning shots of fresh-baked bread of all forms (at the original screening, bread smells were orchestrated through the theatre's ventilation system)

Evans, G. (1992) 'Research on Human Environment Relations', available online from: www.human.cornell.edu/che/bio.cfm?netid=gwe1

Finkel, C. (1984) 'Where Learning Happens', *Training and Development Journal*, Vol. 38, No. 4, 32–36.

Fulton, R.D. (1991) 'A Conceptual Model for Understanding the Physical Attributes of Learning Environments: creating environments for effective adult learning', *New Directions for Adult and Continuing Education*, No. 50, 13–22

Gallagher, W. (1994) *The Power of Place*, Harper Collins

Gilbert, A. (2008) *What the Nose Knows: the science of scent in everyday life*, Crown

Gilbert, D. (2006) *Stumbling on Happiness*, HarperPerennial

Green, J. (1992) *Making Mad Machines*, Gloucester Press

Hall, E.T. (1963) 'A System for the Notation of Proxemic Behaviour', *American Anthropologist*, Vol. 65, 1003–1026

Heerwagen, J., Kellert, S.R. and Mador, M. (2008) *Biophilic Design: the theory, science and practice of bringing buildings to life*, Wiley

Heiss, R. (2004) *Feng Shui for the Classroom*, Zephyr Press..

Horist, L.P. (2005) *The Acrapulator's Guide*, Authorhouse

Hunkins, F. (1994) 'Reinventing Learning Spaces', Speech to the American Center for Architecture and Education, May, available online from: www.newhorizons.org

Itoh, S. (2001) Children and the Physical Environment in School Settings. Report to Danish Building and Urban Research Institute, Hørsholm, Denmark

Jarman, A. (2007) *The Communication Friendly Spaces Toolkit*, The Basic Skills Agency

Johnson, R. (1973) 'The Effects of Four Modified Elements of a Classroom's Physical Environment on the Social-Psychological Environment of a Class', Unpublished doctoral dissertation, Oregon State University

Kopko, K. (2008) 'The Effects of the Physical Environment on Children's Development', *Newsbrief*, Cornell University, Department of Human Research, available online from: www.human.cornell.edu/che/HD/ Outreach_extension/upload/Physical-Environment-Evans.pdf

Lackney, P.J. and Jacobs, J.A. (2002) 'Teachers as Placemakers: investigating teachers' use of the physical learning environment in instructional design', ERIC ED 463645, available online from: http://eric.ed.gov/ERICDocs/ data/ericdocs2sql/content_ storage_01/0000019b/80/19/f5/4f.pdf

Lopez, B. (1989) *Crossing Open Ground*, Vintage

Loughlin, C.E. and Suina, J.H (1982) *The Learning Environment: an instructional strategy*, Teachers College Press

Maxwell, L.E. (2007) 'Competency in Child Care Settings: the role of the physical environment', *Environment and Behaviour*, Vol. 39, No. 2, 229–245

Murray, K. (2003) 'Senator Hopes to Clean Dirty School Bathroom', *Oakland Tribune*, 22 May, available online from: http://findarticles.com/p/ articles/mi_qn4176/is_20030522/ ai_n14548858/

Oldenburg, R. (2005) *The Great Good Place: cafés, coffee shops, bookstores, bars, hair salons, and other hangouts at the heart of a community*, Marlowe & Co.

Pest Press (2006) 'Clutter Control', Issue 1, 1

PriceWaterhouseCoopers (2003) *Building Better Performance: an empirical assessment of the learning and other impacts of school capital investment*, Research Report No. 407, Norwich, Her Majesty's Stationery Office

proteacher.net (2008) 'The Cluttered School', available online from: www. proteacher.net

Purdue University (2002) Reducing Pest Problems in Schools by Reducing Clutter, available online at: http://extension.entm.purdue. edu/schoolipm/Al/PDF%20Files/ Cutter5_9.pdf

Purr, J.C. (2001) Training programme

Reay, D. (1995) 'They Employ Cleaners to Do That: habitus in the primary classroom', *British Journal of Sociology of Education*, Vol. 16, No. 3, 353–371

Robert, G. (2001) 'The Difference is Amazing', *Responsive Classroom*

Newsletter, Vol. 13, No. 1, available online from: www.responsiveclassroom.org/newsletter/13_2nl_3.html

Saeki, Y., Fujita, M. and Sato, H. (1995) 'The Status of Strategies in Learning', Series Manabi to Bunka, Vol. 1, 16

Schneider, M. (2003) 'Linking School Facility Conditions to Teacher Satisfaction and Success', National Clearing House for Educational Facilities, available online from: www.edfacilities.org

Spence, C. and ICI (2002) *The ICI Report on the Secrets of the Senses*, in Association with Oxford University, ICI Publishing

Sullivan, K. (2004). 'The Art of Your Room: what your classroom says about you', *The Art Education Magazine for Teachers*, Vol. 103, No. 10, 30

Taylor, A. (1991) 'The Ecology of the Learning Environment', New Horizons for Learning, available online from: www.newhorizons.org

Ulrich, C. (2004) 'A Place of Their Own: children and the physical environment', *Human Ecology*, Vol. 32, No. 2, 11–14

Vernon, S. (2006) Newcastle Research, available online from: www.ncl.ac.uk/press.office/press.release/content.phtml?ref=1043400783

Walter, D. and Chislett, H. (2001) *Organized Living*, Conran Octopus

Weinstein, C. (1979) The Physical Environment of the School: a review of the research, *Review of Educational Research*, Vol. 49, No. 4, 577–610

Weinstein, C. (1981) 'Classroom Design as an External Condition for Learning', *Educational Technology*, Vol. 8, 12–19

Wolfe, S. (2006) *Your Best Year Yet! A Guide to Purposeful Planning and Effective Classroom Organization*, Teaching Strategies

Wollin, D.D. and Montagne, M. (1981) 'College Classroom Environment: effects of sterility versus amiability on student and teacher performance', *Environment and Behavior*, 13, 707–716

Further reading

Ackerman, D. (1992) *A Natural History of the Senses*, Vintage

Berliner, H. (1999) *Enlightened by Design*: Shambhala Publications

Brand, S. (1997) *How Buildings Learn*, Orion Books

Buckley, J., Schneider, M. and Shang, Y. (2008) 'Fix It and They Might Stay: school facility quality and teacher retention in Washington, DC', *Teachers' College Record*, Vol. 107, No. 5, 1107–1123

Bunnett, R. and Kroll, D. (2000) *Transforming Spaces: rethinking the possibilities*, Child Care Information Exchange

Caine, R. and Caine, G. (1997) *Education on the Edge of Possibility*, ASCD

Darragh, J.C. (2006) 'The Environment as the Third Teacher', ERIC ED 493517, available online from: www.eric.ed.gov

David, T. (1979) 'Students' and Teachers' Reactions to Classroom Environment', Unpublished doctoral dissertation, University of Chicago

Department for Children, Schools and Families (2006) *Learning Outside the Classroom Manifesto*, Ref. 04232-2006 DOM-EN, DCSF, available online from: http://publications.teachernet. gov.uk/eOrderingDownload/LOtC.pdf

Department for Children, Schools and Families (2007) *Sustainable Schools: primary*, Ref. 00777-2007, DCSF, available online from: http:// publications.teachernet.gov.uk/ eOrderingDownload/3676%20 SSTR%20Intro_SEC.pdf

Department for Children, Schools and Families (2007) *Sustainable Schools Teaching Resource: secondary*, Ref. 00778-2007, DCSF, available online from: http://publications.teachernet. gov.uk/eOrderingDownload/3676%20 SSTR%20Intro_SEC.pdf

Department for Children, Schools and Families (2007) *Strategic, Challenging and Accountable: a governor's guide to sustainable schools*, Ref. 00445-2007 BHT-EN, DCSF, available online from: http://publications.teachernet. gov.uk/default.aspx?PageFunction=do wnloadoptions&PageMode=publicati ons&ProductId=DFES-00445-2007&

Department for Children, Schools and Families (2009) Top Tips to Reduce Waste in Schools, Ref. 00368-2007 LEF-EN, DCSF, available online from: http://publications.teachernet.gov.uk/ eOrderingDownload/00368-2007- revised.pdf

Dixon, A. (2005) 'Space, Schools and the Younger Child', *Forum for Promoting 3–19 Comprehensive Education*, Vol. 47, No. 2/3, 51–60

Ellis, J. and Strong-Wilson, T. (2007) 'Children and Place in Reggio Emilia's Environment as Third Teacher', *Theory into Practice*, Vol. 46, Issue 1, 40–47

Evans, G.W. and Hygge, S. (2007) 'Noise and Performance in Children and Adults', in Luxon, L. and Prasher. D. (eds), *Noise and Its Effects*, Wiley

Evans, G.W. and Lepore, S.J. (1993) Nonauditory Effects of Noise on Children: a critical review, *Children's Environments*, Vol. 10, No. 1, 31–51

Evans, G.W. and Maxwell, L. (1997) 'Chronic Noise Exposure and Reading Deficits: the mediating effects of language acquisition', *Environment and Behavior*, Vol. 29, No. 5, 638–656

Evans, G.W. (2006) 'Child Development and the Physical Environment', *Annual Review of Psychology*, Vol. 57, 423–451

Ford, D.Y (2005) 'Creating Culturally Responsive Classrooms', *Gifted Child Today*, Vol. 28, No. 4, 28–30

Fraser, J. and Barker, P. (2000) S*ign Design Guide*, Sign Design Society and the JMU Access Partnership

Fulton, R.D. (2006) 'A Conceptual Model for Understanding the Physical Attributes of Learning Environments', *New Directions for Adult and Continuing Education*, Vol. 1991, No. 50, 13–21

Gerlach, J.M. and Rinehart, S.D. (1992) 'Can You Tell a Book By it's Cover?', *Reading Horizons*, Vol. 32, No. 4, 289–298.

Gleick, J. (2000) *Faster*, Abacus

Greenman, J. (2006) 'Wonderful Walls', *Exchange*, No. 168, 62

Hall, E.T. (1966) *The Hidden Dimension*, Bantam Doubleday Dell

Hall, E.T. (1988) *The Silent Language*, Bantam Doubleday Dell

Higgins, S., Hall, E., Wall, K., Woolner, P. and McCaughey, C. (2005) *The Impact of School Environments: a literature review*, Design Council, available online from: www.designcouncil.org.uk/Design-Council/3/Publications/The-Impact-of-School-Learning-Environments/

Honore, C. (2004) *In Praise of Slow*, Orion

Isaacson, P.M. (1990) *Round Buildings, Square Buildings, Buildings That Wiggle Like a Fish*, Walker Books

Jones, N. (ed.) (1998) *Inspecting the Environmental Dimension of Schools – A Checklist for School Inspectors*, US Council for Environmental Education, ERIC ED 440840, available online from: www.eric.ed.gov/ERICWebPortal/custom/portlets/recordDetails/detailmini.jsp?_nfpb=true&_&ERICExtSearch_Searc Value_0=ED440840&ERICE xtSearch_SearchType_0=no&accno=ED440840

Lackney, J.A. (1996) 'Quality in School Environments: a multiple case study of environmental quality assessment in five elementary schools in the Baltimore City public schools from action research perspective', ERIC ED 432886, available online from: www.eric.ed.gov

Lawson, B. (2002) *The Language of Space*, Architectural Press

March, P. (1990) *Life Style*, Sidgwick and Jackson

Murray, B.P. (2002) *The New Teacher's Complete Sourcebook: Grades K-4*, Scholastic

Palmer, S. (2007) *Toxic Childhood*, Orion Books

Pringle Brandon Consulting (2004) *Post Occupancy Evaluation for Secondary Schools*, School Works, available online from: www.school-works.org/docs/poeFindings.pdf

Royal National Institute for the Blind (2007) *See It Right*, RNIB

Rudofsky, B. (1981) *Architecture Without Architects*, Academy Editions

Salomon, S. (2006) *Little House on a Small Planet*, The Lyons Press

Sang, L. (1994) *The Principles of Feng Shui*, The American Feng Shui Institute

Schneekloth, L. and Shibley, R. (1995) *Placemaking: the design and management of places*, North Pine Press

Shalaway, L. (2005) *Learning to Teach ... Not Just for Beginners: the essential guide for all teachers*, Scholastic

Shoten, I. and Sayeki, Y. (1995) 'Meaning of Learning', *Technology and Disability*, Vol. 13, No. 1/2000, 316–329

Stump, K.H. and Swensen, J. (2005) 'Designing Teaching Facilities Pedagogy as the Driving Force', *Journal of College Science Teaching*, Vol. 34, No. 7, 236

US Consumer Product Safety Commission (undated) *Public Playground Safety Handbook*, Publication No. 325, available online from: www.cpsc.gov

Vernon, S., Lundblad, B. and Hellstrom, A.L. (2003) 'Children's Experiences of School Toilets Present a Risk to Their Physical and Psychological Health', *Child Care, Health and Development*, Vol. 29, No. 1, 47–53

Warner, D. (2005) *Putting the Home Team to Work, Meaning of Learning*, Author House

Wong, E. (1996) *Feng Shui, The Ancient Wisdom of Harmonious Living for Modern Times*, Shambhala Publications

Useful websites

www.accesscode.info – guidance on signage

www.aia.org – the American Institute of Architects: Committee on Architecture for Education

www.anfarch.org – Academy of Neuroscience for Architecture

www.archfoundation.org – national initiative of the American Architectural Foundation (AAF) that seeks to improve the quality of America's schools and the communities they serve

www.bog-standard.org/ – Bog Standard Campaign

www.britishcouncil.org/languageassistant-teaching-tips – teaching tips for language assistants

www.britishcouncil.org/languageassistant-tips-classroom-layout – classroom layout by Jo Budden

www.bsf.gov.uk – official website of Building Schools for the Future (BSF)

www.buildingschools.co.uk – UK school building site

www.cabe.org.uk – Commission for Architecture and the Built Environment: improvement in people's quality of life through good design

www.citizen.org – national non-profit public interest organization

www.cleanup.com.au – Clean-up Australia

www.cpre.org.uk – Campaign to Protect Rural England

www.creative-partnerships.com – creativity and education initiative

www.creative-partnerships.com/projects – school interventions such as de-clutter day

www.data.org.uk – the Design and Technology Association: inspires, develops and supports excellence in design and technology education for all

www.designshare.com – designing for the future of learning

www.drkutner.com – helping parents and professionals make sense of children's behaviour

www.drkutner.com/parenting/articles – helping parents make sense of children's behaviour (Insights for Parents: how do I evaluate a preschool? by Lawrence Kutner PhD)

www.eco-schools.org.uk – improving the school environment both inside and out

www.edfacilities.org – National Clearinghouse for Educational Facilities

www.edrev.org – non-profit organization founded in 1989 to advance learner-centred approaches to education

www.educationforall.com – sustainable building of new schools

www.edvisions.com – helping create and sustain a national network of great small schools

www.encams.org – runs the Keep Britain Tidy campaign

www.english-heritage.org.uk/saveourstreets – English Heritage campaign site for clearing clutter from our streets

www.entm.purdue.edu/Entomology/ outreach/schoolipm – IPM Technical Resource Centre

www.epa.gov – healthy school environments assessment tool (HealthySEAT)

www.eutopia.org – information and inspiration for innovative teaching in K-12 Schools. Part of the George Lucas Educational Foundation

www.freeplaymusic.com – various free music

www.generationhome.org – whole childhood as an agent for spiritual renewal

www.great-ideas.org – Psychology Press/ Holistic Education Press: companies focused on returning balance to education

www.guardian.co.uk/education – School Buildings Must be our Flexible Friends by Les Watson

www.health.state.mn.us/divs/eh/ indoorair/schools/teachers.htm – effective signage

www.hermanmiller.com – research-based, problem-solving approach to design

www.hse.gov.uk – Health and Safety Executive

www.ilabs.washington.edu – Institute for Learning and Brain Sciences

www.infed.org – independent and not-for-profit site put together by a small group of educators

www.innovation-unit.co.uk – Next Practice in Parents and Schools Learning Together

www.K6educators.about.com/od – resource for elementary educators

www.kab.org – Keep America Beautiful

www.kab.org.au – Keep Australia Beautiful

www.kaleo.waianae.k12.hi.us– classroom cleaning controversy

www.keepscotlandbeautiful.org – campaigning work around the issue of litter

www.leading-learning.co.nz – education support and resources

www.learning.luton.gov.uk – tidy game

www.lifeorganizers.com/school-family – one-stop destination for home and office organization

www.livingstreets.org.uk – charity that stands up for pedestrians

www.mayoclinic.org – Mayo Clinic Obesity Researchers' Test 'Classroom of the Future'

www.montessori.org – the Montessori Foundation

www.muf.co.uk – muf is a collaborative practice of art and architecture committed to public realm projects

www.nasuwt.org.uk – UK teachers' union

www.ncacs.org – National Coalition of Alternative Community Schools

www.parenting.com – parenting and babytalk website

www.pathsoflearning.net – features the work of Dr Ron Miller, one of the leading pioneers in the field of holistic education

www.peterli.com/spm– *School Planning & Management Magazine*

www.planeta.com – signage for all

www.preschooleducation.com/scleanup – pre-school education music and songs

www.project-clean.com – resource guides to help schools improve the conditions in their toilets

www.proteacher.net – professional US community and web directory for elementary school teachers

www.psychitecture.com – the relationship between architectural design and psychological variables www.quietclassrooms.org – better classroom environments by reducing noise

www.readingrockets.org/article/311?theme – classroom arrangement

www.responsiveclassroom.org – ideas from teachers using the responsive classroom practices

www.rethinkingschools.org – balancing classroom practice and educational theory

www.cefi.org – non-profit organization which fosters research and scholarly study regarding the impact of school facilities on student achievement and the communities they serve

www.scholastic.co.uk – world's largest publisher and distributor of children's books

www.schoolconstructionnews.com – the online source for design, construction and management

www.schools4life.com – articles and features on building schools for the future

www.schoolzone.co.uk – redesigning the classroom environment

www.suschool.org.uk/ – helping schools to become more sustainable

www.teachers.net – school staff support site

www.teachersnetwork.org/tnli/research/achieve/kihn2.htm – Physical Environment and Student Engagement by Paul Kihn

www.teachingexpertise.com – CPD magazine for classroom teachers and managers

www.teachingheart.net – snapshots of classrooms around the world

www.teachingideas.co.uk – tidy up song

www.teachingtips.com – teaching resources including classroom arrangement

www.teachnet.com – lesson plans, teaching resources, etc.

www.teachnet.com/how-to/manage – getting a head-start on classroom chores

www.tes.co.uk – resources and ideas from the *Times Educational Supplement*

www.tes.co.uk/section/story – Teachers Want a Room with a Brew, by Jonathan Milne

www.toronto.ca/cleanandbeautiful – Toronto, clean and beautiful city

www.tweensandteensnews.com – informative monthly magazine for pre-teens and teens

www.uvm.edu – John Dewey Project on Progressive Education

www.wbdg.org – Whole Building Design Guide: the psychosocial value of space

www.worldtoilet.org – World Toilet Organization

About the author

When I was a girl

I went to many different schools. They varied from cosy Victorian redbrick to new-build comps to gowns-and-flying-chalk grammar. In particular I remember a Brutalistic flat-roofed box set in lovely Suffolk countryside complete with outside pool and girls in navy gym knickers.

However, my memories are less about learning, probably because I didn't do much, than the view from the back row of the many classrooms I inhabited. Here was where well-honed survival instincts enabled me to hide my ignorance and giggle and copy freely. Moving around as regularly as my family did, I learned to evade the new girl novelty phase and aimed to blend in as fast as possible to prevent my academic hopelessness being exposed from day one. This way I thought that when my stupidity did eventually emerge, the humiliation would be short-lived and fairly tolerable as I'd be off somewhere else before long. Seeing an end to it helped me bear any embarrassment and I'd bury myself even more deeply into the trench at the back until I escaped.

Interestingly, from this position I also had the advantage over most teachers. This was even true of open plan builds. I developed a talent for being able to identify the most secure desk with the best vantage point as soon as I entered a room. Once ensconced, I could settle down, supported to the rear by a wall of some sort and with full view of the room to the fore. The position ticked every feng shui landform requirement *and* I could pass sweets.

More than that there was not much to be gained. The classrooms in general stank. Kids sweat, often don't wash and often wear dirty clothes. While I hadn't taken in much in the way of maths or French on my travels, I had been noticing other people of my age and even the odd teacher. I didn't like the smell (of school) but never questioned it, as it was as much a part of daily life as crisps and sweets: floors and playgrounds were always covered with various sticky morsels. Every time I sat down I'd surreptitiously flick over the seat beforehand to rid it of crumbs and check for any other revolting matter. I might have been young but other people's food on my chair or desk made me feel ill. I was only a pupil, however, and didn't think anything further of it, although it was from these seeds of horridness that my passion for celebrating and championing better learning environments grew.

Of course none of the establishments I ever attended sought my opinion on this or any other matter in school. How it was run, where it was run out of, or who ran it, were issues out of my control and I didn't want them anyway. The eventual introduction of school councils made no difference to school environments at all. At the time they were suspiciously viewed by most pupils as an uncool scheme thought up by people who wanted to be our friends when they couldn't. As we saw it, ruling school was their job. Undermining their job was our job.

In the back row I was able to indulge my (now pedagogically validated as vital to creative development) habit of looking out of the window. In retrospect I did this because there was so little else to hold my interest. Even in high windowed Victorian schools I could gaze up at the sky and watch the changing clouds and occasional bird. Once I was nearly rulered for this, although I was more upset at being bellowed at by my last name, a horrible and alienating form of address for any child. All this came as terrible culture shock to a ten year old straight out of the New World Canadian education system. There I was used to huge carpeted libraries with shifting walls; freely available water and being taught outside. There my peers and teachers comprised every nationality and I understood what I was being taught. Of course the school was a wonderful example, perhaps ahead of its time. Everything after we emigrated felt strange and cramped. Space was and still is tight in the UK. Old buildings are poky and more difficult to clean. Sunlight in England is less bright and harder to find. The curriculum was different back then too – at every school. I couldn't understand why *everything* was *so* different. I fell behind in my learning and swept ahead in savvy.

The 70s often seem like the decade when apathy set about the whole country. Things were let go, including schools. People started not to care, assuming someone else would. School classrooms often reflected this limbo-like state of affairs. They were, in general, simply uninspiring, especially to a child ever-ready for distraction. Even at the start of term there was little fresh to grab and hold the attention; no wonder the world beyond the window pane seemed so much more enticing!

Through such an eclectic education I built up my own personal What Not To Do guide to creating respect, humanity and inspiration in school environments. None of it was conscious but, in the same way that some people go into teaching to put right their unhappy school experiences and offer children an alternative to the one they endured, when I grew up I found myself increasingly drawn towards the school buildings themselves and itched to funnel everything I knew into putting them right.

Today this (as I see it) laudable objective is shared by any number of people from architects, academics, designers, psychologists, school leaders and, most fundamentally, teaching staff themselves. Everyone wants to work and learn in the best place possible. Gradually we are evolving towards that situation. In the meantime, this book is intended to help schools make the best of what they currently have. Life and learning is happening right now; no point in waiting around for all your troubles to be solved with a new-build when you could be making your everyday experience a bit better with an on-the-spot clean up. So please, pick the bits of this book that work for you and implement them: make yourself more supported as of this moment.

Index

A 't.' after a page number indicates a table.